skipping stones

a memoir

m.j. blaeser

Disclaimer

I have tried to recreate events, locales and conversations from my memories of them. To protect privacy, in some instances I have changed the names and identifying details of some characters and places in this book.

mb@MelissaBlaeser.com
visit: www.skipping-stones.net

ISBN: 978-1-6570-8196-3
Book design by Victoria Ancone
Edited by Christine Meade

For my husband and my son.

Have you ever watched a stone skip across the water? It moves fast, this is how it keeps from sinking, but eventually, it does—sink.

1| may 2002

When I was thirty years old, I played at dating like I didn't have a lot of skin in the game, or so I liked to say. I had pined for a few guys in the past and hated it--that exposed, out-of-control feeling. Why would I ever chase again? I wanted--*needed*--to be in control to keep disappointment at bay. I needed to call the shots.

When I paid attention, men were easy to read. I knew the ones who would do the pursuing and the ones who needed to be chased. I was not like most women; the things they wanted, I didn't. Marriage and babies had been moved off of my agenda. I wanted a career and I wore that fact like a badge, until I stopped playing at being the tough girl and fell in love.

The night I met Jeff had been one of those long-awaited, warm nights that arrive in Boston in late May. Thursday night at Tavern on the Water--the only waterfront bar in Boston at the time--was the place to be from the start of spring until the end of summer. The Tavern was located on a pier in the Charlestown Navy Yard that offered full city views of Boston. As soon, as it was warm enough, the Tavern opened its sliding glass walls so patrons could spill out onto its wrap-around deck and breathe in the open sea air. The inside had a nautical feel, giving a nod to the decommissioned navy-yard-turned-residential marina. My roommate and best friend Paige and I frequented the Tavern with too much regularity.

The doorman stopped checking our IDs and greeted us merely with, *Good evening, sweetheart,* in his rough Boston accent.

One night, Paige and I were meeting our friend Brad for drinks. We arrived first. We entered the bar and scanned the room for a high-top table, however, all of the glass walls were open, so available tables were sparse. In the corner, I spotted the dark-haired guy whom I had briefly chatted with the previous week.

As we walked by, I directed my gaze to him and slowed just enough to say, "Hey, you're the guy I don't know," with a hint of flirty confidence. Back then, I could conjure up a flirtatious *hello* like a reflex. The previous Thursday, I had seen him at the Warren Tavern, another local Charlestown bar. We had locked eyes in a weird, frozen moment in time--*a movie moment*, a friend would later describe it. He had looked familiar the first time we met, or so I thought, but I couldn't place him. "I think I know you from somewhere," I had blurted out. We had talked briefly, not even properly introducing ourselves. Tonight, he still looked familiar, or maybe I just wanted him to be because he was handsome, like Ralph Lauren, American-yacht-model handsome. He had dark brown hair, chestnut eyes, and a perfectly angled face. He smiled and waved. Paige gave me a glowing smile. "He's cute! You should go talk to him!"

"You mean talk to him again?" I corrected.

"Yeah, go chat him up for real this time," she encouraged. I loved Paige's energy for everything. She had a different I-don't-give-a-fuck attitude than me. Hers was all about never missing an opportunity for fun, whereas mine was, more . . . a fear of not being strong and brave.

"Ah, yeah, no. I don't think so," I said, dismissing the idea.

We found a spot at the bar, perched ourselves on the wooden stools, and ordered our regular drinks; white wine for Paige and a Midori Sour for me. It was green and grossly sweet and I loved it. We began the ritual of discussing work and all of its annoyances, my recent break-up from perpetually-late Lucas, and the details of Memorial Day Weekend in Newport, which was in a couple weeks. A friend had a house just off Thames Street, and we planned to go because we had declared this was going to be the Summer of Fun.

Brad showed up, and he blended in with the general population of white, Irish Catholic males in Boston. He was wearing his Rolex as usual--his hint to the world that he made good money. The watch had been a celebration gift to himself when HotJobs.com had been bought by Yahoo.com. The watch and his Porsche.

"What's going on?" he asked in is his usual slick, almost salesy, way. Brad was an old friend from Connecticut. We had actually gone on a date, maybe two, depending on whom you asked, almost ten years ago. Ironically, I bumped into him in an elevator in Boston and we settled into a mutually-agreeable friendship.

Without missing a beat, Paige chimed in. "I think Melissa should go talk to that guy at the corner table." She glanced in the direction of the guy.

"So, you can stop that," I said refusing to look in the direction of the guy. Brad glanced over.

"Yeah, do it. Why not?" he asked, casually. "Guys do it all the time." He signaled the bartender over.

"Stop making a scene, and no, I'm fine. Really. I don't know him. We have already established this," I reminded Paige, as she had been with me last week.

"Right, but didn't you say it's on your list of things to do before you die--ask a guy out? Now's your chance."

"Do it, Marshall. I dare you," Brad said.

A good number of my male friends called me by my last name, Marshall. I always assumed it was because it suited my *just-one-of-the-guys* demeanor, but maybe it was just a guy thing.

I hated and loved dares. They spoke with very little logic but whispered directly to my "prove yourself" ego.

"Double dare you," Paige added as she looked over at him again. "Oh, he's by himself. Go now, before his friend gets back. It'll be easier this way."

She was right--asking him out would be better to do without an audience. *Take the dare. It's now or never,* the voice in my head said. There was something about this guy; I wanted his attention, even though it seemed I would need to grab it.

I thought of the time I had participated in the AIDSRide, which had been another dare. That was hard for 275 miles and three days; this would be hard for only a minute. Three years ago, in this same bar at just about the same time of year, I had entered into a bet that had been life changing.

"You guys could never do that," Owen said to my co-worker Fiona and me, pointing to the back wall in the bar.

"Do what?" I asked. On the back wall was a poster for the Boston to New York AIDSRide. I looked at Fiona; we had been smack-talking about how we were more badass than Owen, the owner of our dotcom startup. He was always bragging. Fiona and I had taken it as our duty to call Owen out on his bullshit or at least try to put him in his place as often as we could.

"Screw you, Owen," I said, smirking, "Let's do it, Fiona!"

"I'm in," she agreed.

The next day, I bought a bike, and five months later, Fiona and I--along with my childhood friend, Josh--rode our bikes 275 miles with 3,000 other riders, from Boston to New York.

***

On that day, nearly three years later, I didn't know that asking this guy out would end up being one of those life-changing moments. I took a breath and agreed to the dare for the bragging rights. I hopped off my barstool. To say I had butterflies would have been an understatement; I had to fight to keep from throwing up on myself.

As I stood, I adjusted my clingy t-shirt and smoothed my jeans, making sure no bulges showed in places they shouldn't. I was glad I had on my favorite nude, strappy-heeled sandals--they made me taller and my legs look longer. I was still biking a decent number of miles per week, but every little bit helped. Within a few steps, my eyes locked with the guy's--he knew I was coming to his table. *Shit, it's go time.* Adrenaline coursed through my veins giving me the jitters and warming my skin with the heat of embarrassment. There was a fifty-fifty chance I was about to be rejected. Or maybe there was an even higher chance of rejection because if he had been interested, wouldn't he have made a move last week?

"Hi, I'm Melissa," I said. I was probably shaking. I held my breath and tightened every muscle in my stomach to calm the fluttering feeling. To this day, that moment may have been the best core workout of my life.

"Jeff," he said. His smile was easy--not arrogant--and his direct eye contact made the moment the tiniest bit more manageable. Some guys were obvious and awful when you first met them, in the way they looked you up and down, inspecting you. Not hiding that they were assessing your worthiness or, worse, your ability to make them worthy.

"Do you remember me from last week?" I asked.

"I do," he said, holding my gaze.

"Well, I was wondering . . . if maybe you had a business card? I'd like to call you sometime. Maybe go out?" I said, sounding every bit the part of a scared little girl.

The words were out, and, *oh my God,* how unsmooth! That was not how guys asked girls out! I was the loser in a John Hughes movie. Maybe I could leave the bar *right now.* I should have rehearsed something in my head before walking over there. As I stood there in my high-heeled sandals, I suddenly felt like a loser on display wearing stilts.

"I don't have business cards on me but have a seat. Have a drink with me. My friend and his wife will be joining me soon," he said. *Ugh, another female to judge how stupid I sounded. Excellent,* I thought. But still, I smiled. I was here and committed, so I agreed and sat down on the empty barstool next to him. I could see Paige and Brad across from where we sat. Paige had on a giant smile, and Brad was giving me the subtle guy approval—a half smirk that controls a restrained smile. Once seated, it was as if I had just made it to the other side of some vast divide, and I was safely hanging onto the ledge. But the water still felt rough, and I was taking splashes of it up the nose every now and again as I kept replaying my clumsy introduction in my head.

Jeff and I returned to the previous week's *I think you look familiar* conversation until we got to the bottom of it. We may have shared what I call "sliding door moments." Jeff and I used to live in the same apartment building for about six months in the Charlestown Navy Yard. Most people who lived in the Navy Yard took the commuter boat in the morning across the harbor to the State Street dock to get into downtown Boston. Even further back, Jeff went to Yale and would hang out at the Toad, a local New Haven bar. I was not a stranger to the Toad as I had grown up in Connecticut and that bar was well known in southern and south western Connecticut. It seemed plausible we crossed paths.

Jeff had recently bought a condo in South Boston--two blocks from where I was currently living. I joked it was his destiny to keep chasing me. Ian, Jeff's friend returned with his wife Julie. Julie was a bit shy but politely engaged in our idle conversation, the kind that often develops for the sake of a new person--that person being me. I liked how she listened to everyone speak with genuine interest. I liked her ease with herself; it made me less nervous. Ian and Julie were a completely normal, non-scary couple. My fear of being judged dissolved right away.

Jeff gave me his phone number and after a reasonable amount

of conversation and time had passed, I explained I should get back to my friends. I said my goodbyes and returned to my seat at the bar with Paige and Brian.

"Jesus, I'm glad that's over! I never want to do that again in my life--that was awful. I still might be sick," I said, but I was proud of myself and couldn't believe I had just done that.

"Nice job," Paige said, "You seriously have brass balls--that was awesome!"

"Good job, Marshall," Brad added, raising his glass.

2| march 2016

My son Wyatt sat on top of the oversized salvaged wood coffee table, in front of the TV. The coffee table had been bought prematurely for our impending new house. It took up almost all the space in the living room of our small apartment. *He's too close*, I told myself, as I noticed the blue glow and faint hints of green reflecting dimly on his smooth, six-year-old face. If I told him to move back, in five minutes he'd be right back on top of the TV, as if waiting for a magic portal to open up and suck him into the video game he was playing. He was preoccupied for the moment; the requests for me to play Infinity Lego Star Wars were coming less frequently now that my six-year-old had surpassed my playing ability and had deemed me "not a good player." My new status didn't hurt my feelings, but in fact, was liberating in the way only a parent who hates video games can understand.

I sat at the too small makeshift desk in our short-term "luxury" apartment, reviewing the floor plans of our future home. Every time I sat in the designated "home office space" as it was listed on the apartment spec sheet, I felt boxed-in and cramped, in the same way your feet feel after a day of skiing--I needed to bust out of there. It was a small alcove built into a wall at one end of the living room and had a brown-and-beige-speckled Formica desk installed across the width of the opening. The desk was perfectly functional, however, staring at the wall of the alcove only two feet from my face was stifling. I hated this spot--it was where all my motivation died. The apartment was meant to be our home for only six-to-nine months, but it was now approaching a year, with at least five more months to go. It was feeling less short-term by the day. Our previous house sold on day one. The offer had been above asking, so we felt compelled to take it. Now here we were, nearly a year later, with too many of the furnishings from our previous 4,000 square foot house crammed into a 1,200-square-foot apartment, waiting for our home to be built.

In the back of my mind, I knew hating this cream-colored apartment--literally every inch of the apartment was some derivative of cream; walls, carpet, and tiles--was just about perspective. The apartment wasn't much different in size than the Boston condo Jeff and I lived in when we were first married. Many of our neighbors at the time were raising children in similar two-bedroom condos. Was the condo trapping me or was it my life? Our apartment was a corner unit, and it had great light, big windows, big closets, and large bathrooms. I often inventoried this list of positives when I caught myself spiraling into ungrateful asshole mode. I knew I did this; I picked on stupid, low-hanging fruit to belittle or control things that really didn't bother me when, in truth, I was feeling overwhelmed by bigger, harder stuff.

Building a house was turning out to be my worst nightmare. My builder was turning out to be a colossal disappointment, and there didn't seem to be a light at the end of the tunnel. My real estate broker Judy--God love her--had to deal with my endless venting. I wondered if her commission was worth it. I knew I could be demanding and an ass. I wanted building a house to run like building a piece of software; *that* I knew how to control.

I was dumbfounded by the builder's inconsistencies. Some days, his responsiveness had the urgency of a First Responder and the next day all I'd get was crickets from him. The controlling type A person I was brought up to be--and then groomed to perfection in the business world--was wholly insulted by the lack of scheduling and communication. I was sure my builder had an equal amount of discontent for me, if not more.

Initially, building a house was only an idea, but then Jeff and I were looking at land, and the next thing I knew, I was drawing house plans all over scrap paper. That was how Jeff and I rolled--I had an idea, Jeff got on board, and then I was off to the races without a lot of hemming and hawing. I pushed and planned once an idea formed and I could see the outline. I then breathed life into it until the "thing" mobilized. I had been like this all my life; the only difference was, as an adult, I had the ability to actually put things into motion.

As a little girl I can remember how my imagination would take hold of a *maybe* and transform it into reality. My mom would tell me *maybe* she and I could go school shopping together. Time alone with my mom was a big deal for me, and in my mind, I was already at JC Penny, perusing the Garanimal section with my mom at my side, gently sliding my hands down the sleeves and bodices of dresses, examining their softness. I would pick out perfectly coordinating outfits for my upcoming year's wardrobe, and my mom would be equally excited about my choices.

In reality, back-to-school shopping was a disappointing, hurried experience with my three brothers, who were all complaining, as they hated clothes shopping. My mom, trying to manage shopping with four kids in tow, beelined for the sale rack, flicked through the plastic hangers with efficiency--click, click, click--as each banged into each other. She had psychic-price sensing ability; she could sniff out a sale and knew what was outside the budget before I could even lay a hand on it. My tactile experience rarely, if ever, took flight. The red sale sticker always won, preferably a couple of stickers on top of each other, indicating more than one mark-down.

***

It wasn't the apartment that was making me feel cramped. It was other things in my life. The biggest, the state of my once solid marriage. Over the past couple of years, it had become glaringly obvious that Jeff and I were losing common ground. It was hard to pinpoint when exactly it happened, but somewhere between the time I turned forty and forty-four, Jeff and I began to drift apart. I sometimes imagined it like a gradual erosion of land, happening slowly over time. There was no major event, no catastrophic falling out, just the realization that I was lonely. My best friend and partner was falling silent. I could, on my best, most energetic days, provoke and carry our conversations, but largely, I felt abandoned. I had hoped building a house would be a great adventure for us, a project that Jeff and I could work on together. We'd look at pictures on Houzz, share an account with saved ideas, review plans, and pick out finishings together. We needed to communicate more, and we needed something new to talk about, other than our son, so I thought a house would be perfect.

Wyatt was everything to us. There was little I loved more in this world, including my husband, than my son, but the topics about Wyatt were mentally and emotionally exhausting: speech therapy, applied behavioral analysis therapy (ABA), occupational therapy (OT), and individual educational plans (IEPs). This was the language of special needs parents. I spoke most of this coded language now; it had become my wheelhouse. I ran the autism show in our home, providing updates, new ideas, and making plans. Jeff was a great father and cheerleader, but I found myself going back and forth between feeling sick of monologuing about autism and wanting a co-captain. A co-captain would have meant I *felt* there was a shared responsibility for wrong decisions. I could not help but feel like I carried the full responsibility of Wyatt's care, making both the good and the bad outcomes my own.

The divorce rate for couples with special needs children is something like eighty percent, and that statistic was always in the back of my mind. *Be a better team than the rest of them*, I thought. Or, I wondered, were we simply hitting the married-ten-years lull?

I had recently gone back to work four days a week for a private investment firm after a one-and-a-half-year break to be home with Wyatt. I had a better handle on how to manage Wyatt's life, however, balancing it with building a home felt like a self-inflicted middle finger whenever I looked at the house plans. I knew this was my fault; as usual, the reality of my ideas often played out differently than I imagined them. In hindsight, the idea of building a house as a means for Jeff and me to come together was a little like a couple in trouble saying *let's have a baby* to save the marriage. To make matters worse, Jeff had no idea I had concocted this remedy in order to repair our marriage.

At work, things were going as well as could be at a new job. I was glad to use my brain once more and to be back working with a familiar former boss. I had taken a job as a part-time project manager, a role I hadn't done in quite a while, but I liked to believe the skills were hard-wired into my professional DNA at this point in my career, so it would be a piece of cake. Plus, maybe working would bring Jeff and me close again, I hoped.

When Jeff and I first met, he had known me as an independent, in-charge professional. I had been entirely career-minded. Maybe this new version of me was just less interesting to him. In truth, I found me less interesting too. I knew I had obsessed over the world of special needs, and for a period of time, obsessed over my yoga practice, which he had zero interest in. I probably was a snore-fest.

Over the past year and half, I had been struggling to remember how to be confident. The person I had been before suffered from moments of self-doubt, but they were short-lived. On the outside, I had been able to project confidence--I had learned people liked and responded to this version of myself best. I used to run toward hard things. I had built and run a large global team in my previous career. I used to have strong opinions, swore with only minor inflection, and did so unapologetically. I made decisions easily. I just needed to find *her* again.

But that night, pouring through the oversized papers sprawled across my desk, I could not shake the feeling that this house was a mistake. With a colored pen in hand, I reviewed the house drawings and build specification to the contract and the scores of additional email agreements and texts between the builder and me. Our builder seemed to reject the practice of formal change orders and it drove me crazy. Most of my friends complained about their husband's over-involvement in domestic affairs; they had too many opinions and were always bitching about money, but not Jeff and me. We never bickered about money. My youth had taught me a hard lesson in finances, and as a result, I was as conservative in my spending as Jeff. But, on the house project, Jeff had hung back and cheered me on with, "You're doing great. I love it." This annoyed me. *Have an opinion!* I screamed in my head.

Bing! A text from Jeff came in.

Jeff: Dinner?

Yes, that was one of the consistent daily topics we did engage in—*what's for dinner?*

Me: Going over house plans, don't care. No energy

Jeff: Take-out

Me: Yes

Jeff: Where

There it was again; *make a choice!* I could not be the point person for everything in our lives. With every question lobbed at me, my silent storm was building into a tsunami, swelling from the ocean floor, and that wave was about to hit shore and cause mass destruction. I resisted using all caps as I texted back:

Me: you pick

Jeff: Ok Chinese, at Dr. appt still, get it on my way home

I thought briefly about Jeff last night on the couch. I had found him stretched out on the sofa, half-covered with a blanket. He had said he didn't feel well, and his stomach hurt. His forehead had been clammy and hot with fever. Maybe he had Crohn's disease. I remembered an old roommate of mine had suffered from Crohn's disease and she had talked about it being very painful, and her flare-ups always seemed to come at night. Jeff had looked like he was in a good deal of pain, but it was the fever that was concerning. He had texted that it could be diverticulitis. We would know something soon.

I turned my attention back to the floor plans; I was sure something in the master bathroom looked off. Yes, the ceiling wasn't noted correctly. Damn it. I'd make a few more markups then get Wyatt ready for bed. Jeff was not going to make bedtime tonight; this was usually his routine with Wyatt.

An hour had passed and Wyatt was asleep, I was watching TV, and had given up on the house. In the span of this hour, something started to take root in the pit of my stomach. It felt like a distant cousin to hunger, hollowing me out and leaving me nervous—except I knew food would not fill this void--it was worry. The phone rang and it was Jeff.

"Hey," I said impatiently.

"How's it going there? Is Bug asleep? Jeff asked.

"Yea, he went down a while ago. How are you? What's going on? Any news?" I asked I needed to know now.

"So, they found a large mass in my large intestine," Jeff said. He was so matter of fact about it. No worry, in his voice, no quiver, nothing. Not even a pause in his delivery. My head started to feel like it might be detached from my body.

"Did they tell you anything else about it?" I asked.

I knew in the pit of my stomach this wasn't Diverticulitis and my worry bloomed. A mass. Nothing good is characterized as a mass--that is cancer talk. I needed to remain calm and quiet my fears.

"No," he said. "The ER doc is waiting for my doctor to call them back. They sent him the CT scan. I think it's going to be a late night," he said in an even tone. Jeff had already been in the ER for two hours. This was not an infection.

"I'm sorry," he said.

"Sorry for what? You're the one who has been waiting for the past few hours. I can't believe they can't tell you more. This is ridiculous," I said, sounding angry, but my fear was dressed up as anger. I had to pull it together; I wasn't mad at Jeff, but it was so much less scary to be pissed off.

"I'm not going to be able to bring home dinner," he said.

"Oh my God, stop it," I said, laughing in disbelief. Of course he was worried and thinking about me.

"I just wish this wasn't taking so long for you," I said. I knew there was nothing he could do, and I shouldn't make it worse with my own explosive emotions. By the time we hung up, we both were apologizing to each other in the way strangers do who are avoiding an uncomfortable truth.

I got my MacBook from the makeshift desk, sat on the sofa, and started googling colon cancer and stomach cancer. *Prepare and plan,* I told myself; these things had never failed me before. If it is cancer, pray for colon. Colon cancer is the most curable, they say. *Isn't that what they say?* Shit, I don't know. After an hour of googling it seemed that yes, colon cancer had a good cure rate, so I'd prepare.

Jeff called an hour later at 11 p.m. and I was still googling. "I'm not coming home tonight. They are admitting me. They want to biopsy the mass first thing in the morning," he said.

There it was again. That damn word. *Mass.* Of course he wasn't coming home, but hearing it, I began to see time draw out before me and disappear. There was suddenly an abrupt line through my life that I had stepped over. Before and after the *mass*. I was stepping into an unknown with steep ledges.

"I'll be there right after school drop off," I said.

***

I have little memory of getting Wyatt to school the next day. I just remember it was a Friday--my day off. Once I arrived at the hospital, Jeff was sitting upright in bed. Our eyes locked, and I can't recall the steps to him, but the embrace was long and deep. His body was strong and familiar. How could there be something threatening us between our embrace?

"I'm fine," he said when we finally let go of each other and looked back into one another's eyes. I wanted to believe him, but my eyes were already starting to feel wet with tears.

"Okay, let's wait and see what the biopsy says." I smiled. But I was silently screaming, *It's not fine. Look at where we are!* The hospital room was large, meant for two patients, but only Jeff occupied it. Jeff squeezed my hand, and I could sense he was thinking endlessly, always protecting me. I wanted to tell him I was strong, but I wasn't sure I believed it.

"Have you talked to your parents yet?" I asked switching into my "do and manage" mode.

"No. I didn't want to worry them until we know the results," he said.

"What?" I asked. "No. You need to call your parents. They need to know what's going on. Didn't your dad have colon cancer a few years back?" I asked. Somewhere in my memory, it was there, foggy, but I remembered his dad having *something*--either colon or prostate cancer. Maybe this was that; it would be brief and barely memorable and it would be okay.

"I don't know . . . could it have been prostate?" Jeff asked.

"Okay, well, either way, call them right now," I said. I could see he didn't want to worry another person, but there was no way it was a good decision not to tell them.

While Jeff was on the phone with his parents, I sat holding his hand, watching his chest through the blue hospital gown; it moved up and down as he breathed slowly through his words.

"Mom, I don't want you to worry . . . but I'm at Northshore General Hospital," Jeff said in a level voice.

"No, I'm fine . . . they aren't sure. They did a scan last night. It could be diverticulitis," he said.

Oh my God, he was trying to sell that bullshit to his parents! "Jeff!" I hissed, "you need to ask if your dad had colon or prostate cancer. The doctor needs to know!"

"Ah, so a few years ago, did Dad have colon or prostate cancer?" Jeff finally asked. I heard the small vibrations of his mom's voice coming through his phone, but I couldn't make out her words. "They found a mass, too. They are doing a biopsy this morning." Jeff paused, closed his mouth tightly, sealing in his own fear, but a tear formed and ran down the side of his dark-stubbled face. My heart filled with pain, love, and strength for my husband as he fought to keep his composure. Jeff would fight with every last bit of his being to keep his composure for his mother. I reached for the phone and finished the conversation; this was something I could do for him. I could be his strength in this moment.

"Hi, it's Melissa." I sounded confident; I layered my act on top of my inner, emotional shit storm. "Yes, please come. He's going down for the biopsy within the next forty-five minutes."

***

The waiting room was a warm blue. It reminded me of the old office IBM blue of the eighties. The wireless was slow, so I decided to go through the photos on my phone rather than check emails.

There were so many pictures of Wyatt, Jeff, vacations, selfies with me, Wyatt and Jeff, along with random pictures of things I needed to remember to buy for the house or someone else. Behind the perfectly posed vacation photos was an authentically imperfect life filled with a truthful love. As I swiped through each photo in my phone, my mind raced--*what if?* The feeling in my chest and stomach told me I knew there was no *what if*, but *what about the cancer?*

An hour and a half had passed before the western European accented voice broke the quiet of the waiting room. "Mrs. Blaeser?" I looked up and a middle-aged man in scrubs stood at the door, scanning the room. I signaled that I was here and made my way toward the doctor. He ushered me through a door into a bright white room. It was cold compared to the waiting room. The doctor in his white coat in the white room felt clinical. I don't remember the doctor's name--it was hard to pronounce. He wasn't tall like Jeff, but he was taller than me, maybe five-foot, eight-inches. As he looked me square in the face, there was nowhere to hide from his piercing, blue eyes and the truth they were telling me with their kindness. I knew.

"Mrs. Blaeser, everything went very well, but we have confirmed your husband's mass is cancerous and needs to be removed right away." He paused, then continued with more words. " . . . the size of a grapefruit . . . we'll be scheduling the surgery for first thing tomorrow."

"Okay." I nodded. *Okay*--such a short, succinct word, but inside, my composure began to unravel and fight for control over my body. I remember thinking *breathe*, but in that same moment, my tears were winning the fight, arriving first on scene of this disaster. A stream of more words followed from the doctor, but they fell on my ears like a verbal anesthetic, and while each word was probably delivered in perfect medical, technical accordance, they left me a jumbled mess.

Re-entering the blue waiting room, I saw everything was the same, exactly as I had left it. The people were the same, sitting in their same chairs, reading their same magazines, and my coat was exactly where I had left it. But it wasn't the same. Five minutes ago, I worried my husband had cancer, but I had held onto the hope that I was wrong. Now, *I knew* he had cancer.

I sat in my chair, wondering what to do--Jeff would be out of recovery soon. Was I supposed to be sitting here? I couldn't remember what the doctor had said. The room felt small, and I knew my face was showing my emotional cards, my unraveling. I couldn't stop it.

I stood, grabbed my coat and purse, and quickly left the waiting room. The bathroom was just down the hall to the right. I made my way there as fast as I could as *size of a grapefruit* replayed in my head on an endless loop. Nothing described as *the size of the grapefruit* could be characterized as the good kind of cancer.

I pushed open the bathroom door and shut and locked it. In the mirror, I saw a woman who looked like me, but wasn't. My forehead crumpled tightly and my face had turned in on itself. I slid down the back of the door until I hit the floor. Sitting on the hard linoleum of the bathroom, I sobbed, hugging myself. This nightmare was not supposed to be my life. *Fuck, fuck, fuck.*

I exhaled deeply, but nothing changed. *God damn it*, that's all they talked about in yoga: *breathe, breathe, breathe.* But it wasn't helping! I held my breath, trying to shove it down and swallow the fear, to will it to another region of my brain, but it remained. My nose stuffed up and as my breath returned, shallow in depth. My brain felt constricted. I could not think straight; my thoughts reeled out of control.

What does my life look like now? Who will be my best friend? I'm so mad. What about Wyatt? I cannot do this by myself. I told him, damn it. I told him a long time ago I would never survive something like this. I can't do this life by myself. I just can't. You can't die and leave me alone. It's the size of a grapefruit. I prayed to God: please make him better. I promise, if you make him better, I will make our marriage better. We'll live our best lives, just give us more time, please.

I sobbed.

I sat for five--maybe ten--minutes staring at the blue flecks of color in the tiles on the floor; they matched the blue trim on the wall. It felt strange to notice something like that at this moment. But despite the tiles and their distraction, I was still petrified. When I was sure I could not make the fear leave, I got up with this new passenger that had attached to my heart, washed my face, and made my way to Jeff's room to wait for him to come out of recovery.

I expected to find Jeff's room empty, but his parents were there. My tight heart loosened just a bit, and my fear felt a little less heavy. His brother Jeremy was there, too. When I stepped into the room, I felt all of their love touch me and some of the breath return to my body. Jeff's family was my family. I locked eyes with his mom, fell into her embrace, and absorbed some of her strength.

3| july 2006

"Your music is playing. Ready whenever you are," Alicia, the wedding coordinator, said. She looked genuinely excited. I wondered: *Did she look this way at every wedding?* I stepped closer to the windows to look down onto the garden where the guests were seated. Everyone had come. Every seat was full. I knew this, of course, because everyone had RSVP'd, but somewhere in the back of my mind, I had worried.

My mind was always a noisy place assessing and worrying—questioning and trying to play it cool, *just in case.* But today, in this moment, I was floating to the top and rising above some of the noise. I felt like a princess in my wedding gown, despite saying I wanted to be a low-key bride. I couldn't deny it; today I was special and pretty and I loved it. My dress was ivory and strapless. It was made of silk tulle, accented with lace appliqué and a ruched bodice. I wore diamond stud earrings and a borrowed diamond bangle bracelet from my sister-in-law. I had wanted to wear my late grandmother's cross necklace, but I had misplaced it before the wedding. In its absence, I couldn't bring myself to wear anything else. My bare neckline was further emphasized by my hair, which had been pulled back in a low ballerina knot. My grandmother would have loved my wedding and seeing me in my gown. We had shared a special bond when I was a little girl; she knew how I adored pretty clothing and she had been a big part of creating and feeding that joy. When I was young, she used to sew me beautiful dresses before the start of every school year. The two of us would spend the day shopping for patterns and the perfect fabric. When all the work was done, I would put on a fashion show of my grandmother's sewing achievements. I don't know who lit up more--me or her. As I watched the last of the wedding party walk down the aisle and take their places, I smiled. Here was another version of a fashion show and in my mind's eye I saw my grandmother's face light up.

My dad was happy for me--I could see it in his eyes--but nervous too. I was his only daughter, finally getting married at thirty-four. Thirty-four was old by southern standards. My southern-raised parents were married at nineteen and twenty-one. They had probably started to believe my proclamations that marriage may not be for me. My dad looked handsome in his navy blue blazer. He was slighter in stature than I remembered him when I was a young girl, but I think childhood memories do that; they make everything bigger.

My dad extended his crooked arm to me; Alicia's cue to open the door. Stepping from the cool, air-conditioned house, we were greeted by the warm summer evening and the sophisticated, wispy sounds of the string quartet. Mozart's "Sonata in A" meandered through my ears and heart, making me feel light. The first time I heard this piece, it melted into my soul, like falling in love. In high school, I had taken music appreciation, and that was where Mr. Hermans, my teacher, introduced a bunch of teenagers to all the greats like Mozart and this piece in particular. Sitting in a dark, windowless classroom, we were taught to hear, identify, and experience music. Classical music became my secret passion as a teenager, which was odd for a girl who also loved Fugazi and Depeche Mode. But classical always transported me, quieted my mind, and launched my imagination to a greater, more inspired future.

I looked at my dad and he straightened. We were ready. I breathed in the music and felt it pull my body forward. I was here in this moment, on the edge of something beautiful and amazing, about to begin the best part of my life.

We paused at the back terrace overlooking the lake and horseshoe-shaped garden, which was blooming with wildflowers. The day was overcast, which meant we had hit the New England summer lottery, as it was, after all, July. Longer, hotter, and more humid days were to be expected.

Six months earlier, I had stood in the same spot looking at a blanket of snow, curious if the flowers really would fill in, trying to imagine this day. I had worried if the lack of shade trees over the garden would be regrettable in July.

Having the wedding at Jeff's parents' house was the perfect idea. I knew without question this was where we would be married once my mind had started dreaming it. And our wedding in the middle of the garden was stunning. Just outside the terrace door, sat a pile of neatly stacked programs, waters, and Japanese sun umbrellas. My inner voice chastised my younger brother who was supposed to hand these out to the guests. His job and his inclusion in the ceremony was one of the things my mom and I had argued about, and now, five months later, we were still not on speaking terms. *Let it go,* I told myself as I lifted my eyes and found Jeff's gaze. He was standing at the edge of the golden tiger lily flower beds, looking deep in thought, but then he smiled when he saw me and I exhaled. The groomsmen--Jeff's two brothers, Jeremy and Ben, and my older brother, Gabe--were in navy blue blazers, pink and cornflower-blue striped Brooks Brother ties, and khakis. The bridesmaids--Paige and Laura, two of my closest friends, and Miranda, my sister-in-law--were in periwinkle chiffon gowns finished with pink peony bouquets. I had to admit--it did look pretty damn good. I loved when I got something right; it was like the surprise of Christmas morning when what you hoped to get is actually there.

My father and I began to walk. We came to the steps that spilled down onto the grass, and I gathered up my dress so I wouldn't trip, revealing my white J. Crew flip flops. I wondered if they were still a good idea. We descended the few steps into the garden and my choice of flip flops was quickly confirmed as a good idea as soon as we hit the soft grass. No spiky heels sinking into the ground for me. As my father and I walked toward Jeff, something shifted in me. At first, it was subtle, then it was a swell that filled my chest and threatened to break my perfect bride composure with a flood of tears. I breathed slowly and intentionally through my nose. If I opened my mouth to take in too much air, my face would have turned into a giant, ugly cry.

I loved Jeff. I could have let go of my father's arm and ran to him. I didn't need vows. I had committed to this choice in my heart long before this day. As we continued to walk toward Jeff, I saw him see me. He had always seen me for who I was and who I had been in order for me to become the person in this moment, walking toward the rest of our lives. Jeff was my best friend. It wasn't that I needed him--I *wanted* him in my life. I wasn't sure I was good enough for him, but I was going to try. I had gotten lucky, and now I had to be grateful.

With every remaining step, I held my breath, swallowing my emotions. Standing in front of Jeff, he smiled and quietly said, "You look beautiful. I love you." Jeff, always my reserved guy of little words, made the ones he did say count.

The ceremony had short, typical vows, nothing off script. Our justice of the peace had inquired about making it longer with various prayers and rituals, but none of it rang true to who Jeff and I were. In truth, it was difficult to plan a longer ceremony that would have too much family involvement when my mom and I had not been on speaking terms for most of my engagement. I considered how whatever choices I made would almost certainly drive the wedge in deeper between my mom and me. Our falling out was weighing on everyone, especially Dad. In our conversations and emails, he always expressed how upset he was by what had transpired, but my mom and I were stubborn women and we each thought we were right.

The week before the wedding, I stood in my future mother-in-law Sylvie's kitchen doing a lousy job of holding back tears. I was stressed putting together all the wedding pieces. Work had been busy as usual, and a deep dread was growing in me expanding in size with each passing day as we moved closer to the wedding.

"If you haven't already planned something, I'd be happy to have a brunch at the house the day after the wedding," Sylvie offered. All I could think of was how my mom would see the brunch as a way to make her look bad. My relationship with my mom could be unpredictable--I couldn't get it right. "Oh, that's so generous of you, but . . . we're fine. Really. We can skip it. It just feels like a lot," I said.

"It's no bother. Really," said Sylvie. I couldn't tell whether she really wanted to host it or if a post-wedding brunch was something she felt needed to be planned. Her generosity was something that I never knew how to process. It made me feel uncomfortable, but also delighted--like a light that finds you, but then you quickly become embarrassed by the attention.

"I know, thank you. I'm sorry. I'm just a little stressed," I said feeling the shake in my voice as I spoke.

"Why are you stressed? This is a happy time!" Sylvie smiled with a bit of confusion.

I had been holding this in for months. My mom had not come for my bridal shower, and my elusive "she couldn't fly in" was all I gave for an explanation. I suspected she knew my mom and I weren't best friends like she was with her daughters, but saying the words out loud had a way of bringing the truth to the surface like a permanent resident that could never be evicted.

"It's . . . it's just my mom and me. We're not talking and we haven't been for a while. I don't want her to feel like I'm cutting her out of all the planning," I said. My words were abridged compared to what I was really feeling: deep embarrassment. The Blaesers didn't carry on with each other like this, not speaking to each other for five months. Why hadn't we, why hadn't *I*, just ended it? Why did we always get so damn mixed up? The truth was I was always ready to go toe-to-toe with her when it came to throwing stubborn down.

Sylvie looked me square in the eyes and past my embarrassment. "That is the life and family you had; you had no choice. You and Jeff are the family you choose," she said and hugged me.

***

Sylvie and my mother walked to the front of the garden where a table had been set up with a candle. The candle was a unity candle symbolizing a joining of our families. I watched the two of them light the candle. Both of them were smiling and my mom appeared a little nervous. I wasn't mad at her anymore, but I wasn't really sure I could tell her that yet. My thoughts returned to Jeff who stood across from me, so handsome and serious. I loved him. He was my *home* where I finally belonged. Within ten minutes, my choice to begin and create a life with Jeff was sealed and officiated. Jeff and I completed our vows--we had become one. We were married.

4| march 2016

I sat in a small, upholstered chair near the Starbucks in the hospital lobby. Morning sun filled the entire café. I needed to call my mom. What would I say? How would I start? I hated dramatic conversations with my mom. I always wondered if I should temper how I was feeling, take it down a level, say less. I looked at my phone, pressed *Favorites* and selected "Parents." The line rang twice and mom answered.

"Hello!" she said.

"Hi . . . it's Melissa." My voice shook and I knew that little waver would tell the story of my heart. My mom would know.

"Melissa, what's wrong?" Mom asked, her tone was urgent and serious.

"It's Jeff." My voice broke. "He has colon cancer," I said through tears. I couldn't hold it in. This was a difficult call. Needing my parents had never been an easy thing for me to admit. At forty-four years old, I still carried old stories created from old wounds. And my armor of independence and self-reliance had kept me safe from potential disappointment. But right now the armor was heavy, and I wasn't sure I could keep up the front. I was afraid.

"Oh God, Melissa! What?" Mom gasped.

"I know, it's awful," I said, looking down at my lap.

"Where are you? When did you find out?" Mom asked.

"I'm at the hospital. We're waiting for Jeff to come out of

recovery from his biopsy. Mom . . . they said the tumor is the size of a grapefruit." I took a breath, hoping the air would fill my body with the strength to continue talking. "They scheduled surgery for Sunday to remove it," I said.

"I'm so sorry, Melissa. This is awful. What can I do to help? If there is anything let me know. I can come to Boston," she said.

"No, it's okay," I said reflexively. "But, thank you. I appreciate that. Right now we're just waiting to see what's next." I was lost. I probably needed help, but I didn't know what to ask for or how to accept it.

"God, this is such a shock. I feel so sorry for you," said Mom in a soothing voice. *Feel sorry for me.* This snapped me out of my quiet tears. I knew she loved me and cared immensely about what was going on, but I would not have anyone pity me. In a flash, my anger and stubbornness conspired to stifle my sadness and I was me again. My defensive self was called to stand on the front lines of my feelings. I heard my mother's words and not her intent.

"Mom, I'm sure it's going to be okay. I just wanted to let you and Dad know what was going on." I paused. "I should get back to Jeff's room in case he's back from recovery." We ended the call with *I love yous*.

I did love my mom, but I didn't know how to lean on her.

***

When I returned to Jeff's room, the TV was on. The volume was like a barrier between us and the growing tension, but none of us were really watching.

"Why is it taking so long?" Joe asked.

"I wonder if he's still in recovery," asked my brother-in-law, Jeremy. We were all concerned that Jeff wasn't back yet. Every approaching sound in the hallway made our eyes dart to the doorway. Even the quiet walkers passing by the room caught my attention. Did they have news?

Occasionally, I shared a glance with Jeremy, and his smile said it all: "I'm here." This was Jeremy's way. As the eldest of six kids, he tried to take care of everyone--an extension of his parents. Jeremy seemed to have decided to live the 90/10 rule in all aspects of life. I first learned of and became indoctrinated to the 90/10 rule on my wedding day.

5| july 2006

Earlier on our wedding day, I had been stressed that if you looked closely, you would have seen all the ways I had half-assed the celebration. I had Scotch-taped together the parts that overwhelmed me. I had a wedding planner, but I had failed to use her help in the ways I should have. The guest tables had been named for things significant to Jeff and me, but I didn't include a sequential numbering system so people could easily find their tables. I had forgotten to let people know that they were meant to use the restrooms in the house and how to find them. Missed details like this plagued me like a loud, pounding voice.

"Jeff, I feel awful," I said, pulling him aside the day of the wedding. Everyone was running about setting up his parents' home for the wedding and reception, which would take place in just a few hours.

"We haven't thought of a way to include your dad." My dad would be walking me down the aisle, the mothers would be lighting the unity candle during the ceremony, and his dad would be sidelined. I shuddered. How could I have forgotten?

"He's fine. He won't care and I'm sure he won't even notice," Jeff assured.

"But I'm not comfortable," I tried to emphasize. I had this nagging feeling of being ungrateful. In my life *ungrateful* was like the eighth deadly sin. There were times, like this one, where I found myself needing, *wanting*, to express gratitude because I was keenly aware I had been the recipient of generosity in a way I had never imagined. Jeff's parents had opened their home to us for this wedding, and I had not considered how to include both of them in the day's events. I was on the hook for this. I paused for a bit of thinking. "Okay, I think I got it. Would your dad feel comfortable saying grace before dinner?" I asked.

"I'll ask him, but I'm sure he'll be fine with it," said Jeff.

"Okay, let him know it doesn't have to be anything crazy, and please apologize for us, for me being so late on this, and I'm sorry for not asking sooner."

"It's fine--trust me," said Jeff.

"Okay. I have to go to the hair appointment now with the girls. Thank you," I said, kissing him.

Hours later, Joe, Jeff's dad, stood in the middle of the wedding reception tent before all of our guests, confident, sure, but without airs. I saw in him the man who addressed many boardrooms. He had a confident and easy presence; he pulled you in and made you want to listen. Everyone under the tent leaned in to hear him speak. Jeremy, Jeff's brother, had toasted us before with the kind of humor that had the guests leaning back in their chairs laughing, especially my friends at Jeremy's assuredness in his vision that we would have many children. Anyone who knew me for more than a day knew children were questionable.

Joe was graceful. My new father-in-law thanked our guests for coming to our family's celebration, and he warmly invited everyone into his home. He talked of the marriages in their family before Jeff and me. This was not "the dinner time grace" I thought of a few hours ago; this was better. I was impressed how he was so easy in addressing everyone as if he had practiced this. I leaned in to listen.

"There is a rule I like to tell all my kids about when they get married--it's the secret to a happy marriage. I think, *I hope*, some of them will know what I am about to say," he said with a playful smile. I looked at Jeff, who smiled with a knowing roll of his eyes. His siblings smiled and their eyes brightened--they knew exactly what was coming.

"I like to call it the 90/10 rule. It's really very simple." He paused. "In marriage, if you give 90% and expect 10%, then you will always be happy. This goes for both spouses. If you are both always giving more than you expect you will always be happy."

Jeff leaned into me. "My dad does say this at all the weddings."

I smiled. "I love it," I said. And I really did.

6| march 2016

Joe stared at the clock on the hospital wall. Standing as if to walk out, he said, "It has been a while. You'd think Jeff would be out of recovery by now." I saw the growing concern on his face, but his tone was even. He was the father and the husband--he would not give in to panic. Joe held true to his 90%; he would give his best show of strength for his family.

Finally, a nurse appeared. "Jeff is having some pain. We've given him something for it and are keeping him in recovery until it subsides. It shouldn't be much longer." She gave a sympathetic smile to our wide-eyed pleas for more information and then left.

I looked at the clock--it was almost time to pick up Wyatt from school. I had not anticipated--or maybe I did and refused to accept it--that this day would be my undoing. I should have lined up help sooner. The day had gotten away from me.

"I need to get Wyatt," I said.

"I can go," Sylvie volunteered.

I wanted to accept the help, but Sylvie was Jeff's mom, and I couldn't deny this is where she needed to be. We all needed and wanted to be here. My 90% would be to honor her as his mother. We would both be mothers at this moment in the ways that were required.

"No, it's fine. I need to arrange a babysitter and I'm coming back as soon as I can. I won't be long," I said, trying to sound in control like this was a regular day. Hugs, kisses, and *I loves yous* were exchanged and I was out the door.

Once in my car, I looked at my phone and saw my brother had called. I pressed the start button on the ignition, turned on my seat warmer, and waited for the heat. I took a deep breath and exhaled, watching my breath floating in the frigid air. March. I hated New England weather. I pressed the *Call* icon on my screen next to my brother's name and exited the hospital parking garage.

"Hey, what's going on?" he answered.

"Um . . ." I paused.

"Well, I'm not doing so great." My voice gave way to a teary inhale. I held my breath, trying to pull my emotional pieces back inside as they were about to spill out.

"Are you okay?" he asked. Gabe was my older brother. He was in California and I wished he lived closer. All of my life, I had a bumpy relationship with my parents, but he was my constant. I looked up to him.

"No . . . I'm not." I paused as I drove. "Jeff has cancer," I choked out, then took a breath and held it in until the prickly sensation of sadness filled the inside of my nose, and I again re-ordered my emotions to keep my shit together.

"*What?* Oh my, God," he said.

"I know," I said. I gave into some of my tears then sniffed back the remainder and got back on point.

"When did you find out?" he asked.

"This morning. Well, I had a feeling last night, but we found out this morning." I explained the events of the past twenty-four hours as I drove south on 128, only slightly aware of nearby cars.

Over the years, my brother had become not just my touchstone but a good friend. Growing up, Gabe had always been this heroic figure to me--"the chosen one," as my friends joked, because it always seemed that he was the family favorite. I didn't really mind. I agreed he was funnier and smarter. Gabe was the one who gave my parents a reason to brag: honor roll, private schools, and the University of Southern California for college. And then the great job. My dad loved that Gabe was a COO and CCO for a hedge fund. "Do Mom and Dad know?" he asked.

"I talked to Mom this morning. She was pretty upset."

My mom had been truly shaken by the news and she wanted to be a help, but there was nothing I could think of I needed from her in Tennessee. Having a somber call with my brother or mother was strange as our family was not overly emotional with each other. If felt awkward, like when you go to hug someone, and you both choose the same side. Great intentions but still a bit bumpy. I knew Gabe was concerned for me, he always was, but he showed concern in the same way my dad did with next steps and directives. Gabe was a paler version of my dad, but I couldn't fault him for this--I was cut from the same cloth. Whenever Gabe or I became too aggressive or salty in our demeanor, I would tell my sister-in-law, "That's the Marshall coming out," referring to my dad. My dad was the "honest one," as he liked to say. He told you like it was. My mom, on the other hand, was silent but deadly--she could freeze out a snowman and in the next breath, want to be its greatest defender.

Despite feeling as if I was constantly in a struggle with my family to be "the boss of me," I was always able to share with Gabe what was on my mind, and he was masterful at helping me decouple from the tangle of my emotions. In spite of the years of big brother/little sister incidents--like the time he cut one of two of my pigtails off--we were alike. We both tried like hell to be perfect and in control of our lives. He was winning at it for sure, but our wiring was similar.

In an awkward lull of silence I broke in, "Colon cancer is the best cancer of all the cancers to get, so we're really lucky in that." I needed to bring the conversation back up to a manageable emotional level.

"I have heard that," said Gabe, matching my optimistic tone.

I ended our call composed and promising updates because I couldn't leave my brother feeling like I was about to break apart while he was sitting in California.

Rise, I thought, and find your strength.

***

I was almost home when my phone rang, but I couldn't reach my purse. The call went to voicemail; I would listen as soon as I got home. But then the phone started ringing again, and again, it went to voicemail. I pulled off to the side of the road, feeling a little panicked. This was not the kind of day that I wanted to miss two calls in a row.

I pulled into the town hall parking lot, grabbed my purse, and rummaged for my iPhone. I had two voicemails; one from an unknown number and the other from my brother-in-law, Ben.

Ben was a doctor and his voicemail explained in accessible medical terms that emergency surgery was needed for Jeff in the next couple of hours. I should come back to the hospital as soon as I could. During the biopsy, the tumor had perforated. Now the grapefruit-sized tumor was two tumors, and they were spilling cancerous cells further into Jeff's body. *Shit*, I thought, many times over. The next voicemail was from the surgeon, Dr. Cornbloom, giving a more technical version of the same message Ben had left me, but with a very clearly worded directive: get childcare and come back.

I called my friend Ashley. "Hi, Ashley, can you do me a huge favor?" I asked, immediately feeling the uncomfortable burden of asking for help. I hated asking her to babysit, as I was sure it was the last thing she wanted to do. She was a speech pathologist and worked with little kids all day, and now I was asking her to come to my house and babysit my sometimes-behaviorally-challenged child.

Ashley and I had talked earlier in the day. She knew the storm that was brewing; she had listened to one of the first rounds of panicked sobs. Ashley had become my version of "phone-a-friend." She and I became close during our yoga teacher certification and my hip surgery. Ashley had a way of showing compassion without the pity; she saw my struggles, the ones I shared and the ones I wasn't comfortable talking about, but never called me to task on them.

"Of course," she said, "do you have more news?"

"Sort of. I don't completely understand what's going on, but Jeff needs to go in for emergency surgery right now. The hospital called me to come back. Do you think you can meet me at my place and watch Wyatt? I'm picking him up from school now." With each word my heartrate picked up speed.

Ashley, unwavering as always, responded as if I had asked her to pick up a gallon of milk for me. "I'll meet you there," she said with ease.

I made one more phone call to Kathryn, Wyatt's old nanny. Between Ashley and Kathryn, Wyatt would be cared for. I sighed a breath of relief and gratitude, and at the same time, I was as exhausted as if I had been awake for a week.

***

When I arrived back at the hospital, I went to the pre-op suite where Dr. Cornbloom had directed me to go in her voicemail. Jeff's family crowded around him and spilled out of his blue-curtained area. As soon as they saw me, a space at Jeff's bedside parted. The morphine had kicked in, and Jeff was finally out of pain from the biopsy. He looked stoned, which was a relief because I couldn't have stood to see him in pain. We held hands as his parents and two brothers filled the space around his bed. I tried to look composed, but mostly I was holding my breath and clenching my stomach. I tried to keep my fear sealed up inside, but its presence was clinging to me like newly-formed skin.

"I love you," Jeff said.

"I love you, too." I blinked back tears.

"Don't worry. I'm fine," said Jeff.

So typical, I thought. *You're not fine; none of this is fine.* Jeff looked old and young at the same time; his hair fell in his eyes like I imagined it probably did when he was ten-years-old, straight and unkempt. But I could also see how tired he was. Several years had worn on his body in the course of hours.

The doctor came in and gave an update about the tumor perforation, concern of micro-cancer cells spreading, surgery plans, and how the tumor had breached the abdomen wall.

"Would you like to see the imaging?" she asked.

"Yes," Ben said.

"No," I said. "'ll stay with Jeff."

I couldn't leave him, and I couldn't bring myself to see "the mass." The idea of it made me dizzy. I hated the tumor.

Jeff seemed small to me--all six-foot, three-inches of him--and, for the first time ever, breakable. How and when had this transformation happened? It had only been hours since I had hugged his sturdy body.

Around the corner, Dr. Cornbloom and Ben quietly discussed the tumor and some details of the surgery. I tried to tune it out and stay present with Jeff for as long as I could. "We're going to be fine," I said, squeezing his hand.

"How's Wyatt?" he asked.

"He's fine. Ashley is with him now, and Kathryn will be over later. I'm going to tell him you're on a business trip, okay?" I asked. I knew this was where his mind was going.

He smiled. "Good idea."

I didn't know how to talk about this with Wyatt since he was only six years old, too young and immature to understand. Being on the spectrum changed how we considered and planned presenting new information to him. Usually I researched best practices, consulted his various therapists, discussed a plan with Jeff before we pulled the trigger. But this situation was going to be a game-time decision.

It wasn't long before the surgeon was back. The nurse and anesthesiologist were busy with charts, checking and rechecking Jeff's personal information. They were efficient and, within minutes, dismissed us. It was time. I bent down to kiss Jeff's forehead, which was cool and his skin felt looser than I remembered. I prayed to God this would be remembered as only a tremulous chapter in our growing-old-together process. "I love you," I said and smiled.

"I love you, too."

"See you when you wake up," I said. I squeezed his hand and stepped away from the side of his bed to make room for his mom and dad to give him their love. I stood at the foot of his bed and watched his mother will her strength onto her son. Sylvie was a force. "I love you; you got this," she said. I imagined her encouraging him as a little boy, the personified version of Dr. Seuss' *The Places You'll Go*. She was why Jeff was so strong. I walked back to the waiting room with Jeff's family; the walk felt hollow and unsteady and I could not have felt more alone. Jeff was my partner in life; he was supposed to be by my side for the moments of joy and the hard, scary ones. Walking away from him felt like walking away from a part of myself. My head swam with the *what if*s and I could feel parts of me batten down the hatches, preparing for a storm. I told my mind to move to the front seat and my heart to the backseat. *Just figure out how to get through tonight.* The surgical suite waiting room had an electronic board with color-coded blocks indicating status, containing patient ID numbers. You could watch the status of your loved one's surgery change as they moved through the various stages of pre-op to recovery; it reminded me of a chart I might have created in order to give project status at work. I made a cup of coffee, sat across from the board, and let my mind drift.

Why had I wasted so many days being pissed off and disappointed about nothing? Had I become just another boring, miserable housewife? This was not the life I imagined. I had once thought I would live an uncommon life. I'd blast that song by Jewel, "Life Uncommon," and believe it in my soul. *Just believe in a life uncommon, and it will be brilliant and memorable.*

Jeff and I had started out as uncommon--I had asked *him* out, and I had been the first one to say *I love you.* We rarely fought, and frankly, what was there to disagree over? And then we got married--another thing I thought was not for me. Marriage had seemed like such a bad idea--why would I ever let anyone think they had control over my life? Worse, why would I give up my dreams for anyone else? These were ideas I had written in my head as truths from what I had seen growing up and from previous relationships. But that all changed with the realization that my heart chose Jeff before I could even put words to it to call it marriage. I wanted to be with him forever and if the world was bent on calling that marriage, so be it; we'd just paint our version a color that suited us. Neither of us imagined changing the other's dreams. Independence was equally important to both of us. Everything pointed to the universe aligning us as a perfect match. We would be better than the rest; I really thought this. But here I was with my self-pity party and the truth that we had become pretty damn ordinary over the past few years. Common bickering over the dishwasher, common growing distance. I didn't even want to consider the eighty percent divorce rate within the special needs community. Forever was meant to be for *forever.*

I stared at Jeff's patient ID number; it comforted me and tricked my head into thinking there was some control bestowed upon me by staring at the status board.

We were the only ones in the waiting room. It was dinner time; most people were probably well into their meals by now. I kept the patient status board in my view and joined my in-laws' conversation, holding onto my cup of coffee as if it were something important. Jeff's brothers, Jeremy and Ben, recalled stories of hockey camp when the three of them were kids.

"We did push-ups in the parking lot on broken glass," Ben said with a mix of shock and tough pride.

"Come on," Sylvie said, in the way a mother can always sniff out an exaggeration.

"It's true," Jeremy agreed.

"JJ will tell you," Ben said.

Joe gave a playful eye roll and I laughed. We had been waiting a few hours at this point for progress on Jeff's surgery. The storytelling was a welcome distraction, and I always loved envisioning Jeff with his brothers as kids. It felt like being let in on a fun family secret.

The three boys had grown up playing hockey from the time they could walk, and they played through college. Jeff had been exceptionally gifted and was drafted into the NHL by the Penguins. However, no matter what successes Jeff had had in life, he would be JJ, the little brother, who was now bigger than both Jeremy and Ben. The Blaeser brothers were something like what brothers were in the movies; handsome, loyal, best friends, and insular. Watching others try to attach themselves to a brother as the best friend was almost like watching a hopeless girl think she could break up a life-long marriage. These brothers were the three musketeers.

It was getting late, and I didn't have babysitting coverage through the night, so I would have to leave soon. Leaving sounded awful. I should have done a better job finding childcare. Another wife would have done a better job.

"I'm going to need to leave soon and relieve my sitter," I said to Sylvie.

"It's fine; I will be here all night if they let me stay," she said, without any hint of the judgment I was putting on myself.

"I'm sorry. I wish I could stay," I said.

"You have to take care of Wyatt. Don't worry," she said. I knew she meant it, but I wanted to be better than how I was showing up. Sylvie had arranged for my sister-in-law, Jeff's younger sister, Chloe, to come to the apartment tomorrow to watch Wyatt so I could be at the hospital. She knew how to make proper, reliable arrangements.

I drove home in a fog still revisiting our life's memories, not nearly enough of them yet. We had created some great moments, but there were still so many more I was counting on. We had so many places to see.

7| november 2005

I sat in the snug corner of the sectional, scanning my endless queue of emails, when one from Gateway Vacations caught my eye: "Italy for Thanksgiving" was the subject line, which sounded like a great idea to me. I looked up from my laptop across the room to Jeff. He was in the kitchen--the beauty of the open-concept floorplan.

"Jeff, what would you think about going to Italy for Thanksgiving?" I asked and even as I asked, I knew it was more of a statement than a question.

"Um, I don't know . . . don't they watch fútbol over there and not football?" he asked, with a bad imitation of an Italian accent. I rolled my eyes.

"I'm sure Fútbol Americano will be on in a bar or on cable in the hotel," I said.

It didn't take much convincing--Jeff was in. We were going to Italy for Thanksgiving.

Jeff's passion for travel was about a five on a scale of one-to-ten. He had traveled a lot when he played hockey, and I always felt he had lived a whole different life when he was younger. Jeff had been an elite athlete. He had played on the Junior Olympics team and played hockey all over the world. Unfortunately, Jeff's hockey career ended prematurely due to injuries and too many knee surgeries. Jeff always said airplane seats were not made for people his size. He was right--when the passenger in front of him put their seat back, the hard tray table would press against his knees. One knee, the damaged, hockey-career-ending knee injury still gave him a good deal of pain.

The night before we left for Italy, we were at Jeff's condo settling in with take-out and CSI. Jeff was opening the Italian food; chicken and broccoli for me, chicken parm for him. "So, listen, if we get to check-in really early tomorrow, we can request exit-row seats," I said. We were scheduled to fly out of Boston on an early evening flight. I had it worked out that if we arrived at Logan airport maybe forty-five minutes early, we would be there early enough to request exit-row seats. I couldn't stop thinking about Jeff having to squish into a seat for six-plus hours to Rome with his knee throbbing. I wanted him to have extra room so he wouldn't be miserable for me.

"Got it," he said turning on the TV.

"So be packed early." I added, to make sure he really *got it.*

"Check," he said as he slid the CSI Vegas DVD into the player.

***

The next day, my morning took a shape of its own. I should have never opened my work email. By the time I looked at the clock in my apartment it was 11 a.m. and four hours had sped by. I had to drop my car off at the body shop. I had been in a fender bender the week before, and I was going to leave the car for repair while we were away. I called Jeff to say, *Let's leave now.* The repair shop was on the other side of Boston. I still needed to pack--and fast--so we could check-in early and hopefully get exit-row seats.

Once we dropped my car off, I hopped in Jeff's silver BMW, settled into the passenger seat, and buckled my seatbelt.

"Okay," I said, "Now let's get back fast. I'll pack, and we can get checked in!"

"Done," he said.

"What? What's done?" I asked.

"We're checked in," he said "Exit-row seats. Done." He smiled.

"Wait, when did you do this? Did you call? They never let you call anymore." I was confused and impressed. Had he smooth talked them?

"Nope, I went to Logan last night," he said. Again, I was confused.

"When?" We had watched CSI until pretty late.

"At midnight," he said.

"Oh my God, why did you do that?" I laughed, shocked.

"You wanted exit-row seats. I figured it was important to you," he said.

"It was, but for you," I said.

I smiled. My heart felt hugged and, in the same moment, my chest seized up. I knew I might cry. Who was this person? *Because it was important to you*--these words fell on me so gently. I couldn't remember the last time someone said these words to me or did something for me for that reason.

Jeff was everything I never knew I wanted. I was never able to answer the question, "What are you looking for in a guy?" And it never seemed to matter. I did know what I didn't like, but these things always seemed obvious; liars and mean people were out. Then Jeff came along and every time he did something wonderful or loving it was like tasting a new food I didn't know I liked. *Yes, that! I want that!*

I was feeling like such an idiot--only a week ago, during our last CSI binge, I had had a selfish meltdown over our impending engagement. We had been talking a good deal about marriage and had looked at rings, so naturally I was thinking about it. My girlfriends had asked me several times if I thought Jeff would propose in Italy. I didn't know. Maybe it would be one of those romantic movie moments in front of the Trevi Fountain or at the Spanish Steps I thought, but at the same time I doubted Jeff would ever do something that public. It stressed me out--not knowing what to expect.

So there we were, settled in for *another* episode of CSI and I got into my head. Jeff I am sure was in his own pre-show world. He was likely wondering what Gil Grissom and his team of CSIs would be faced with in the next episode, when I took a deep breath and conjured my *I got this* inner attitude.

"So, I have this thing on my mind I need to talk to you about it," I said.

"Okay," Jeff said. He reached for the remote and paused on the opening credits.

"This trip to Italy—you know I pretty much planned the whole thing, and I don't mind that I did," I said, feeling a little nervous, "so, I just want to make sure you know that if you were planning on proposing in Italy, you can't. Because then I would have planned my proposal." I paused. "I know it sounds crazy, but we've been talking a lot about rings, and I just think this is important." I knew I sounded crazy and presumptuous, but I had to say it because it really would have been all wrong. I couldn't tell people he proposed on the trip I planned. I had to manage my expectations and be responsible for my happiness.

"Okay, got it. No proposal in Italy," Jeff said with an air of lightness.

I was being proactive, I mused. High maintenance, but self-maintaining: that was how I justified my behavior to myself. I could never let go and just trust my happiness to someone else. It was too risky.

Jeff hit play on the remote and the familiar Who song "Who Are You?" continued with the opening credits.

8| december 2005

Like clockwork, Jeff was waiting in his car at the entrance of the T stop where I could clearly see him. Jeff had made a habit of picking me up at the end of my day since he was out of work and it was December and the weather had turned colder.

During my ride from Downtown Crossing to Andrew Square, I oscillated between pissed and panicked. My day had sucked. My job was killing me. How much longer could I keep it up? I had been at the software consulting firm for two years as a project manager and by now I expected I would have felt more . . . capable. But I couldn't shake the feeling that I sucked. Lately, it had gotten so bad that I had given into the feeling that I had no idea what I was doing. I was tentative all the time. I had never been overly confident on this client account because I believed I had to work harder at it than others in order to keep up. I didn't really mind the hard work, but it could be exhausting at times. It was the subject matter; this kind of finance had always been a stretch for me. I hated feeling like the dumbest person in the room. No one had explicitly said or indicated to me that I should *feel* stupid, but I did. I regularly second guessed myself after I spoke in meetings wondering if I could have done better.

On this particular day, Kameron, one of the relationship leads on the account, gave evidence to my inner voice. The day ended with a scolding, or so it felt like it. Kameron had requested a "quick call" with me and I knew this meant feedback. Everyone at the consultancy was fond of and expected to give each other—solicited or not—feedback all the time.

Kameron did not mince words.

"You are not managing the client. You need to do better," he said. He was clear and I knew what he meant. His words cut through me and I bit down on the inside of my mouth so I wouldn't cry and embarrass myself. I didn't disagree, but I didn't know what to do. I listened to the rest of my feedback: push harder, take control of the meetings. I sniffed.

"Are you crying?" he asked.

"No," I said, horrified. *Screw you Kameron* I thought. But Kameron's question was what I needed--it pissed me off enough to pull my shit together and complete the call.

Of course, Kameron was right. I wasn't doing a great job. I hated working with and being around this client. He was a creep who always made me feel disgusting; the too close sitting, the up-and-down stares. How could I explain all this to Kameron? Paired with all of my mounting insecurities, I was afraid Kameron would think it was a cop-out if I told him how creepy the client was.

I got in Jeff's car feeling as deflated as a week-old balloon. Everything about my current situation made me feel trapped and pissed off.

"How was your day?" Jeff asked.

"Awful, I hate Kameron," I said.

"He thinks I'm not strong enough with the client," I said.

"Well, you're off for a week, it's Christmas time now, so you won't have to deal with him or the client for a bit. Let's forget it for now. Want to go get some food?" Jeff asked. I considered telling him about the creepy client, but now wasn't the time. Maybe I was too sensitive. I stared out the window because I didn't want Jeff to see how upset I really was.

"Okay, I'm starving," I said. "Can we please go somewhere

that serves more than the usual pub fare? I'm so sick of shitty bar food."

"Sure, do you have a preference on where you'd like to go?" Jeff asked.

"No," I sulked.

"Okay, maybe a walk first to get rid of the day. It's pretty warm out. It'll help you unwind," Jeff suggested.

It was unseasonably warm for December 24th. The temperature had reached sixty-five degrees, which was uncommon for New England.

"Yeah, that's a good idea. Where?" I asked.

"How about Castle Island?" he suggested.

Castle Island was a five-minute drive from Andrew Square. It was pretty there at night. I had never really paid much attention to the fort. I was usually running around it and immersed in my "Run Hard" playlist. But on this night, I noticed how the lights that lit the walking perimeter added a warm glow to the park. The fort, while it was historically a point of protection, was not nearly as imposing as you would have imagined. The park, which had been built around the fort, softened the hard corners of the stone walls and made it feel serene. I started to forget about my awful day. The ocean air and still of the night was working; I was coming back to Jeff and me. What did work really matter anyways? It was just a job.

We walked holding hands. Jeff talked about how he walked out here regularly to think and clear his mind. I knew he did this; it was one of his daily rituals for the past few months. I imagined him walking and listening to sports radio, and it made me happy. Over the past four years of dating, I had come to know Jeff as he had me. I could imagine his days and the routines he fell into. We had become a *we*. I thought in terms of the two of us. I considered how my decisions affected Jeff. I loved him deeply and he had become the ground under my feet, the thing I had craved all of my life, but never knew to call *the feeling of being home*. We walked until we made it to the back side of the fort, facing the ocean. It was quiet as we were the only ones out there. The night was unusually still; typically the winds came off the ocean and across Castle Island so hard it could make even walking a workout. Jeff stopped walking, faced me, and asked how I was feeling.

"Better," I said, sighing out any remaining stress from the day. And he hugged me, pulling me in tight. A short hard edge jabbed against my ribs. My mind clicked and my heart jumped.

A small square box!

Jeff was talking. I heard his words, but I couldn't hold onto them. I was still trying to register the moment, when my mind finally caught up. Jeff said, "I love you; will you marry me?" An open box rested lightly in his hand, just between us.

"Yes!" I said.

With something between a smile and a nervous laugh, I closed my eyes, buried my face in his chest, and hugged him again. I looked up at Jeff and he smiled. We met in a light, playful kiss. Jeff pulled away slightly, removed the ring from the box, and slipped the two-and-a-half-karat solitaire on my finger. It was beautiful and delicate. The band was encrusted with diamonds and shimmered in the night lights. The band was too big on my finger, so I closed my fingers tightly to keep it secure as we walked. I didn't want to take it off.

I would remember this day as perfect.

As we headed back to the car, holding hands, we talked about where to go for dinner. "Well," he said, "I guess Tavern on the Water is out. Crappy pub food and all." Jeff laughed and wrapped his arm around me, pulling me in closer as we walked.

Feeling the weight and size of the ring on my finger, I was ashamed of my earlier behavior. "I'm sorry about the rant. I have just been in such a mood because of work," I said. Jeff squeezed my shoulders tighter, and I leaned into him as we walked.

"It's okay," he smiled. "You pick. The Tavern would be sort of weird now. I had planned on proposing there."

Tavern on the Water is where we had met; where I had awkwardly asked him for his number; where it all began.

"I'm sorry, shit. I'm really sorry," I said. It seemed that I could never filter at the right moments.

***

Wedding planning started slow. Getting married felt surreal. I knew Jeff felt a bit tentative when it came to setting a date since he was still out of work. But what did it matter? I had a job. I hated it, but it was a job. Somewhere between talking about locations and cost, we agreed on a wedding in six months at his parents' home. The engagement was short, but we had dated for four years.

In February, my mom came up to Boston from Tennessee to work on wedding planning with me. It all went well until it didn't, and I was in cold-shoulder land, our age-old cycle of conflict. I was fourteen years old again.

Since leaving Connecticut at the age of twenty six, I had kept my life neatly partitioned from my parents. In Boston, I was in charge of myself and I felt less judged. Growing up, all I dreamed of was getting out of my tiny town and out of my parents' heavily rule-based house. I wanted to live a life that felt important even if it was to no one else but me, and I didn't want to hear shit about it. However, the inescapable truth was this: my family and I couldn't help playing long established roles with each other and the reflex to do so was strong, like muscle memory. Pair those behaviors with years of beliefs and stories, true or not, and, well, even the best intentions don't stand a chance. After my mom's visit, I called her from work to see how her flight home went. I was at a client site with very little time or privacy. My dad answered, which was not typical. When I asked to talk to my mom, he hesitated.

Something was up.

"Ah, I'm not getting involved. I'm going to let her tell you," he said. I then heard the distant sound of him telling my mom to take the phone.

"Hello?" said Mom, her tone flat.

"What's wrong?" I asked. "Are you mad at me?" I already knew the answer.

"Well, I had time to think about it on my flight home, and I wrote my thoughts down," she said in a clipped manner.

"Okay, do you want to tell me what you wrote?" I asked, already feeling and hearing myself armor up.

"I have a list of reasons why I'm upset with you," my mom said.

"All right, well, let me know what they are." I was trying to sound open, but I knew my teenage-practiced and finely-honed attitude was seeping through the cracks. *Here we go*, the ticker flashed in my head.

"You embarrassed me when we were wedding dress shopping. You knew I was going to pay for the dress and you made a big deal of paying for it yourself. Your friend Paige saw all this in the bridal shop. She gave me an awful look for not paying after she overheard the whole conversation. Also, how come no one in our family is in the wedding party? And Jeff's family will have more guests at the wedding than we will."

My mom's list had a few more minor offenses, but these were the big ones. I became defensive and furious as I memorized her words, readying my attack. Any willingness I had to listen with openness dissipated like a speck of water on a hot stove.

"Mom! Paige is practically deaf, for real. She didn't have hearing aids in at the shop, so she didn't hear anything. You would have had to be literally standing in front of her face for her to hear you." I was fired up. "And, I paid for the dress because I picked an expensive dress and didn't want you to worry about it. Me paying for the dress had nothing to do with making you look bad," I spat out, mustering all the restraint I had in me. I really wanted to unleash.

Trying to be financially responsible was blowing up in my face. I was proud of the fact that I was taking care of this, but I didn't tell her that, I just unloaded on her. I didn't *hear* what she was really trying to say, and she didn't hear what I didn't tell her. That had been--and would be--the theme of many arguments between my mom and me. This particular phone call didn't go on for very long, but the argument did.

When I told Jeff the story, he was somewhere between shocked and confused. His family didn't have dynamics like this. His sisters, on their worst day, would never have dared challenge their mom in this way. I wondered if he now saw in me a side that concerned him, but he didn't. Jeff was sorry that my mom and I had this kind of relationship. It prompted me to share more of my childhood with him, about how my mom and I were no strangers to the epic fight turned into marathon cold shoulder competition. This fighting tactic had existed in my house since childhood, and I had grown accustomed to it. My mom and I would argue, stop talking, and then just one day, Mom would decide it was done.

In the end, my mom and I fell into an unspoken agreement that we would be comfortably cordial to each other at my wedding, but we didn't really speak to each other until after the wedding, six months later. Neither of us tried.

9| march 2016

Returning to our little apartment from the hospital didn't offer the relief of coming home I had hoped for. I knew this was only a rest stop as Jeff was still in surgery. No news had come through on my drive home.

The warmth and familiar smells of home greeted me as I entered the quiet apartment. I could tell Wyatt had been fed chicken fingers. Wyatt would be fast asleep by now. Kathryn was waiting for me with a look of love and concern. Almost immediately she got up from the sofa and hugged me tightly.

I could be myself around Kathryn, sloppy and imperfect. It always struck me funny that this was the case, as I was about fifteen years older than her, but her soul may have been older than mine. When I first met Kathryn, interviewing her to be Wyatt's nanny, I knew I liked her. Her genuine joy seeped through her in a way that washes over you like the warm glow of something beautiful. I knew Kathryn was the right person to care for my baby. Years after I met Kathryn, I met her mother, Carmen, and she was the same--all warmth and heart. They seemed to have love genetically wired into them.

Kathryn's kindness reached out to me and it wasn't pity or sadness. I knew she was sad; I saw it in her red eyes, but it was her own sadness because she and Jeff had become close. I allowed myself to release some of my tears, and she cried, too. Kathryn knew my heart; she had become part of our family over the years. She had nannied for Wyatt from ages one-to-five. The years that mattered. Kathryn had potty-trained Wyatt, taught him the words to "Rolling in the Deep" as she bathed him, and had been a part of teaching him to communicate with Jeff and me. In those days, we all learned his picture exchange communication (PECs) and baby sign language. But moreover, Kathryn was his first example, outside of Jeff and me, of every day unconditional love.

Kathryn opened a daycare with her mom once I decided to leave the consultancy and become a full-time mom, almost two years previous. I could not have imagined a better career for her. She would love any child in her care.

We sat on the sofa and I updated her with as much as I knew, which wasn't very much. Mostly, I said a lot of *I don't knows*.

"Jeff is going to be fine," Kathryn said. "He's so strong."

"I know... you're right," I said. "It's just all so sudden." I sniffed, looking up at the ceiling as if there was an answer to all of this there.

"I know," Kathryn said. "I'm still in shock, too."

"I just don't know what to think," I said. At that very moment my mind was swimming.

"Rest, you just need rest," Kathryn said.

"You're right. I feel like it's been weeks and it's only been a day."

Kathryn and I talked for almost an hour before she left. I had kept her far longer than I should have. I surveyed the apartment. What do I do now?

Jeff's socks were on the floor of our bedroom where he always left them. God, he is messy. I laughed and cried a little, tears of uncertainty rolled down my cheeks. I took a shower to wash away the day. The hot water washed over me, the day replayed in my mind on an endless loop. My most selfish thoughts crept through me in the secret alone space of my shower. My worst fears were shouting at me: how would I raise Wyatt on my own if it came to that? Jeff was supposed to be my everything, the family I chose—my home. Things had been off lately, but he was my person and my forever, forever was not this short. The weight of these thoughts collapsed my chest and broke apart my sense of certainty in everything. We belonged. I panicked, where did I belong without Jeff? The tears came, washed down my face and got lost in streams of water. The shower was the perfect place to cry; no one would see or hear me here.

The feeling reminded me of my trip to Peru that included a five-day Peruvian hospital stay with pulmonary edema, where I had also cried in the shower--full-body, chest-heaving sobs. Five days of IVs, doctors, and nurses who barely spoke English and the voice in my head of Carl Lowes, my co-worker, telling me, "You'll be fine in Peru, just don't get pulmonary edema because you can die from that." Peru had been planned as a girl's trip to hike to Machu Picchu. It went wrong from day one when I came down with food poisoning and altitude sickness. I was hospitalized right away. I was not able to breathe without being hooked to oxygen; my lungs filled with fluid and I was drowning myself. I was scared to death, and for five days, I focused on the picture of Jesus Christ guiding a surgeon's hand that hung on my wall. *The hand of God*, I thought. If JC *was* giving a helping hand, I wanted him to do something about my veins that were clotting at the I.V. site. The nurses had to keep finding new spots to run my I.V. Not only was this painful, but I was starting to look like a junkie. As soon as I was cleared, I jumped a train to the ruins, met up with my friends, and joked about all the weight I lost and the needle marks on both my arms from my hospital stay. I never mentioned my tearful breakdown in the hotel shower the night before.

I toweled off from the shower and Kathryn was right: I needed a good night's sleep. Before I got into bed, I picked up my phone one last time and saw I had received a voicemail while I was in the bathroom. My brother-in-law, Ben, had called to say Jeff's surgery had gone well and the tumor had been removed. Jeff was in recovery, resting, and we would be able to see him in the morning. I sighed a breath of relief. I would see him tomorrow, and the new chapter in our lives would begin.

10| march 2016

I awoke the next morning alone in my bed. Jeff was missing. There was no warm body next to me taking all the blankets. In his place was the knowing that our world was tilting. It wasn't long before I heard Wyatt talking to himself and bumping around the apartment, pulling all of his toys out. The familiar sound of plastic toys banging on the wood table came next. It was time to get up.

I looked at the clock on the stove. Chloe, Jeff's youngest sister, would be here soon.

"Wyatt, Aunt Chloe is coming over. She is going to spend the day with you," I said. trying to sound cheery and excited.

"Where's Daddy?" Wyatt asked from his train-covered play table that had been set up in the dining room.

I smiled and my stomach sank. "He's on a business trip. He'll be home soon."

I handed Wyatt a cup of milk with a straw. "Okay," Wyatt said. He paused. "More jelly toast?" This was one of three things that he would eat for breakfast.

The apartment felt smaller today and everything about this space was getting on my nerves more than usual. Wyatt's toys were strung from one end of it to the other with a mixture of Legos, Angry Birds stuffed animals, Superheroes, and the occasional book. We should have leased a house--another misstep by me. The new house was supposed to be done soon--at least that's what they kept telling us, however, I knew by looking at the lot and the condition of the build that soon was a relative term and it wasn't going to be soon enough. I had driven by the house a couple of weeks ago, and while it was in progress, there was nothing about it that looked "soon" the roof wasn't even on yet. This whole house-building process had sucked, but now that Jeff was sick, it went from first on my list of the worst experiences to a constant annoying buzz. But I didn't want to think about it now; the house or the builder. I needed to focus, get dressed, and get myself to the hospital.

***

I walked into Jeff's dimly lit room. He was awake; groggy but awake. I was relieved. I didn't know exactly what to expect, but what I saw was better than I had feared. We'd be able to talk and I needed to talk to him, to feel him back in my life. Last night, the version of him I saw was frail and faded and it had scared me.

"Hey," I said as I walked over grabbed his hand and kissed him on the forehead. I was afraid to hug him. I hadn't seen the incision on his abdomen yet, but I could guess it was an aggressive one. I didn't want him to move.

"I love you," I whispered.

"I love you, too," he replied.

How was it we were here in this moment? We had been sucked from our life of typical disconnection after nearly ten years of marriage to this alternate place of life-altering uncertainty. The scariest truth was this: we hadn't simply woken up one day and Jeff suddenly had a giant cancerous tumor in his body--it had been growing for maybe eight or nine years. It was that big. That knowledge made my mind reel. Was it his shitty diet? Was it me? Did I, or our life, stress him? Was it environmental factors?

Jeff looked tired. "Ben left me a message last night," I said. "Everything went well, they got it all." I hoped this would bring him relief.

"I know. Dr. Cornbloom was here earlier. She'll be back, but she briefed me a little," he said with a tired smile.

We both fell silent and I knew we were both thinking *thank God*, but something kept us from saying it. We just smiled and, I nodded and held in a long breath.

"Hello?" asked a cheery voice. Sylvie and Joe walked in with Jeremy, Jeff's brother, on their heels. Each of us had on our own version of the same mask: tired relief. The last twenty-four hours had felt like twenty-four months. We stood around Jeff's bed anxiously looking at him for signs of unexpected fatigue, discomfort, or anything that told us something wasn't right. I didn't know what to do with myself. *What next?* we all wondered. Dr. Cornbloom made her entrance as we were all talking about nothing: Wyatt and school, the house, the apartment.

"Hello, Blaesers," Dr. Cornbloom said. "Jeff, how are you feeling? Still a little sore I imagine?"

"I'm okay," he said.

"Well, we'll keep up the meds to keep you comfortable," she said.

"Do you have any results on the biopsy?" Joe asked.

"Well, it's preliminary, and we need to wait for the labs to come back, but I was explaining to Jeff this morning we are looking at colon cancer. We got a good sample of the margins for the lab, and right now it looks like we are likely dealing with stage four or best case a complex stage three. His case is unique; the tumor did breach the abdomen, and with the perforation, we don't know about the spread of the micro-cancer cells... there are very few cases out there like his. I am still researching it," she said.

There it was.

I had been waiting for someone to tell me how the rest of our lives would look as I no longer felt I had a say. There was nothing I could do. A dizziness swept over me as I heard *four, complex three, unique* in my head. All we could do was wait for the worst or very worst news. I would need to Google more so I could formulate my questions. But I knew enough to know that stage four cancer was nothing to take lightly. My hope for colon cancer--the good cancer--only a short while ago now seemed naïve and wholly uninformed.

"Right now, the best thing you can do is rest," she said, looking at Jeff. "Your body will recover from surgery if you do your part."

"Got it," he said.

"The hospital has Wi-Fi, so bring in an iPad and log into Netflix and catch up on some shows. There are some great ones to watch if you haven't seen them already," she went on, "like *Breaking Bad*. That's a favorite."

I looked at Dr. Cornbloom and then at Jeff. Was she really recommending that my husband, who she just told his cancer looks like stage four, should watch *Breaking Bad*? The show is about a man with terminal cancer who turns to drug-dealing because he doesn't have insurance or money saved for his family. Dr. Cornbloom said her goodbye and Jeff's family excused themselves from the room moments later. I looked at Jeff. "What the fuck was that?" I asked, my nerves and anger were like an emotional shaken soda bottle.

"What?" he asked.

"*Breaking Bad?* She just told you to watch the show about the man dying of cancer!" We had started watching *Breaking Bad* a few months ago.

With something between a furrow and smile, Jeff said, "Oh yeah, I bet she didn't even put it together."

"I hate her," I said aloud. I didn't really; I hated these marathon moments I was trapped in. I didn't care about *Breaking Bad*. I needed to know about this cancer staging. I had read online about stage one, and I had emotionally prepared for stage one in my mind, but deep down my gut had known it was something worse.

Jeff's parents and Jeremy returned. I had never been one to hide my feelings, as my eighth-grade Spanish teacher once told me in disgust, "Melissa, you wear your emotions on your sleeve for the world to see." But I was resigned and leaned up against the wall. We fell back into the idle talk and encouraging comments, but a minute later, we heard the sound of charging rubber soles down the hallway, and suddenly there were three breathless orderlies in Jeff's room. We looked at them wondering if something was wrong with Jeff's equipment and they looked at us. It felt like an odd stare down until one of them asked, "Is everything okay?"

"Yes," Sylvie answered.

"You're leaning against emergency call button," said one of the nurses to me.

I stepped forward, looked behind me, and there was a bright red button on the wall, labeled "emergency." "Sorry," I said.

11| march 2016

Jeff was being moved to his own private room. My exhaustion came and went in quick waves. One moment, I was fully awake and the very next, my eyelids needed to close so badly they hurt. I would make a quick stop at the Starbucks in the lobby and then meet everyone back up in Jeff's new room.

With latte in hand, I opened the door to Jeff's new room, which was bright and his family was already back by his side. I was embarrassed to walk in with my latte as I hadn't offered to get one for everyone else. A true "Blood Blaeser" would have checked with everyone first to see who wanted a Starbucks. Jeff and I had an inside joke that Blood Blaesers were the best Blaesers. If you were a Blood Blaeser you knew the rules and expectations because you had been raised by Joe and Sylvie, so you were already set up to succeed. The in-laws, or "out-laws," as one of my brothers-in-law--who was also an outlaw--referred to us, had to pay closer attention. It wasn't so much that we had been raised poorly or were completely selfish, it was just the Blaesers were elevens on a scale of one to ten. Joe and Sylvie never imposed their will or expectations on others per se, but Jeff and I liked to observe the subtle differences between the Blood Blaesers and the out-laws. "I'm sorry, I should have texted to see who wanted Starbucks," I apologized, feeling awkward as the aroma of my hot latte filled the room.

My family held an undertone of Darwinism. "Learn to take care of yourself" could have been our motto.

"Oh, we're fine. We're not due for our Starbucks for a few hours." Sylvie smiled. It was probably true--I knew that they went through spurts of monitoring their Starbucks intake levels. "This is a nice room," I said. "So bright and a nice view onto the courtyard."

"The VIP treatment for Jeff," Joe said. We all smiled and laughed. Joe had been in this hospital some months back and could not get a private room. Of course, given the chance, there was no doubt this man would have moved heaven and earth for his son's comfort.

I scanned the equipment, the tubes running into Jeff that disappeared under his blankets. The night before, Dr. Cornbloom indicated there was a possibility that Jeff would come out of surgery with a colostomy bag. I hadn't heard it confirmed yet, but I had a feeling this had been the route they had taken. Within a few minutes, the doctor appeared.

"I'm going to check your wound dressing, if everyone could give us some privacy. Mrs. Blaeser, you can stay if you'd like," she said.

"Yes, I'll stay," I said. Everyone left and I braced myself to put on my best unaffected face. I hated wounds, blood, and cuts. All of it made me uncomfortable. The doctor opened Jeff's hospital gown and a mound of gauze covering his incision ran nearly the length of his abdomen. And there, on the lower left side of his stomach, was the colostomy bag. I waited and watched Jeff for a reaction, questions, or any sign of concern. But nothing. Jeff's face was calm, almost blank.

Dr. Cornbloom was pleased with the wound. "The wound looks good," she said with enthusiasm. It was pink and neatly stitched. Dr. Cornbloom went on to explain some rules of thumb for caring for the "ostomy bag." She talked about it as if it was like changing a band aid. Her words weren't measured or strained. They held no pity. I admired this. Dr. Cornbloom assured us that an ostomy nurse would be in shortly to go over in more detail how to care for and change the bag. Jeff continued to hold his face neutral, but faintly in his eyes, I recognized the flicker of disappointment. The colostomy bag was new to him and here were two women, his wife and surgeon, hovering over his body, discussing the mechanics of how his large intestine had been re-wired. Bowel movements would go through this gaping hole and into a bag.

Dr. Cornbloom left the room, the door clicked closed, and I looked at Jeff.

"Are you okay with this?" I asked, trying to broach the subject gently.

"Yes, it's what has to be done," he said. The colostomy bag was necessary until his chemo treatment was completed. Then, once Jeff had completed a series of tests with clean results, they would "put him back together," as Dr. Cornbloom had said. The colostomy bag was necessary--and temporary--in order to get chemo started ASAP, which is what the oncologist had wanted.

"Hon . . . did you know what a colostomy bag was before now?" I asked.

"Nope," he said.

"Okay," I said. "Well, we'll learn more about it when the nurse comes. I'm sure it's going to be fine." I tried to reassure him, but my head swam a bit. Would he let me support him with this? Up to this point in our relationship, Jeff had rarely, if ever, let me help him. Jeff never complained--he barely told me if he had a headache.

Vulnerability was only something I did in our marriage, and it was my version—a bit more *Princess Bride* than, say, *Terms of Endearment*--emotion delivered with humor. This would be a big change for Jeff.

12| march 2016

On Monday, after we made it through the weekend, we learned Jeff would probably be in the hospital for the remainder of the week. The line at the hospital Starbucks was longer than it had been over the weekend. I was surrounded by people in scrubs wearing hospital badges who belonged here. They seemed natural in their conversations with each other.

When I finally approached the counter, my eyes fell on the frequent buyer punch cards again, and this time, I grabbed one. I'd be back a few more times this week. I placed my order of a grande latte and stepped aside to wait.

A few minutes later, I made my way down the corridor to the elevator. As I stepped inside, a slightly older woman followed. She looked anxious, so I smiled and said, "Hi." I didn't typically chat up strangers, but it always struck me as rude how people ignored one another in small spaces.

"Oh boy," she said. "What a week." She sighed.

I smiled. "Tough one? Well, I hope it improves."

"It has to! My husband almost died," she said. "His appendix burst the other day! It was so scary. That's a serious thing you know," she said, holding my gaze.

"Yes, that is scary. Is he doing okay now?" I asked.

"Oh yes, he's fine now, but the scare of it all!" She rolled her eyes to the ceiling.

"Of course. I'm so sorry, but I'm glad that he's doing better," I said.

The woman smiled and seemed lost in her thoughts for a moment. I let the silence sit between us for the remainder of the ride as I stared at the brushed metal walls of the elevator. I didn't have it in me to share my story. I wasn't in the mood for drama swapping. What could I say? *My husband is looking at stage four cancer, be grateful.* Instead, I just smiled.

The doors opened and I looked at her one last time. "Good luck," I said and headed off the elevator.

I opened the door to Jeff's room. Ben was in his scrubs, probably on his way to his practice. We exchanged quick *hellos*, and then he headed toward the door to leave. I followed him out.

Outside of Jeff's closed door, I put my hand on his arm and looked into his eyes. As soon as I did, the rims of my eyes filled with tears. *Oh no, don't cry,* I thought. *That will make him so uncomfortable-- just spit the words out.* I hadn't told Ben how appreciative I was of him. He had been running point on everything medical regarding Jeff's health. He asked the questions that mattered, looked at the medical charts, researched the doctors on the team. I felt helpless on my own, but confident in Ben; he would tell me what I needed to know. "Ben, I need to thank you for handling everything. I don't know what I would do without you." I put my arms around him and quickly hugged him. I could tell he didn't know what to say as I embraced him. This was the Blaeser male I expected--public affection was not familiar territory. Ben hugged me back, smiled, and assured me that everything was going to be okay. I owed Ben so much more than an awkward hug.

Jeff's parade of visitors throughout the day was filled with friends and family. This was no surprise; Jeff was always described as "such a great guy" or "solid." I was sure I was not the girl any of them would have picked for him. Jeff and I joked that I was his alter-ego. Jeff followed rules, and I ignored them or looked for loopholes.

The nursing team who cared for Jeff was gentle and compassionate. They liked him, too. I wondered if he was a rarity for them. I never considered what cancer patients and their families were supposed to look like, but this week, we were the youngest people on the floor. Peering into the open doors as Jeff and I walked the floor for his exercise and rehab, I kept thinking, *we don't belong here. This is a mistake.* Maybe the landscape would have been different if we have been at Mass General where his parents had originally wanted him moved on that first day. Joe and Sylvie Blaeser didn't mess around. Northshore General Hospital was a forty-five minute drive from Boston. But Ben stepped in and assured everyone that the team of surgeons on Jeff's case were capable--he had researched and vetted them and thought moving Jeff was not in his best interest at the time.

This was the Blaeser machine.

No one asked me what I thought. But, at the same time, I didn't mind--we were all thinking only in terms of what was best for Jeff.

***

The calls from my family were steady. My brother called daily to see how Jeff was doing and how I was doing. I didn't have much news, but I was glad to feel the connection with my brother and my family. My brother was always optimistic and encouraging. It reminded me of when he taught me how to ride my bike.

"Come on," he had said, as we walked my newly de-training-wheeled bike up what seemed like an Everest-sized hill. "You'll be fine." Nervous as hell, I climbed on my bike. If he said I could do it, I guess I could. Gabe was my cool, daredevil older brother. I don't remember if I pushed off or if he launched me, but one minute I was staring down my asphalt-Everest with my pink bike under me and the next, I was gliding. For a few glorious seconds, I was riding my bike without training wheels. Gabe was yelling, "Pedal, pedal!" I turned my head to hear him, and with that, I swerved, hit the grass, and wiped out in a ditch. The thing about falling in the ditch was that Gabe helped pull me out. He had run down the hill, yanked my bike off of me, dropped to his knees, and helped me up. I had fallen, but *we* got up together.

***

My dad, on the other hand, when we were kids, he insisted that we get up when we fell. At least this is how I remember it most of the time. But, as my dad aged, I began to see his softer edges. The part of him that was faithful, and it was strong. In his years of retirement, he had re-acquainted himself with God and the church. He prayed for Jeff, for me, and for our family. My dad found comfort in this faith. Initially, it was interesting to understand this side of my father; this was not a side I had experienced growing up. That is not to say my father wasn't a man of faith before, but it had never come up in between his lecturing me for being out late or running my smart mouth. Back then, I viewed people of faith and religion as people of a certain kind of pious perfection. My stereotypical view of a churchgoer had been formed by TV shows or movies like *Footloose*, with the preacher-father who bans dancing. But my father's faith was his guidepost. His religion was not a proclamation of perfection, but his practice to become a better version of himself. To live the life he felt God intended for him to live. He became a regular at his church and an active participant in that community.

I didn't always know exactly which version of my Dad I would get on certain issues--the transformed faithful Dad or the strict "my house, my rules" Dad. And while I finally learned at forty-four years old that neither version had anything to do with me, it was still hard. The memories and occasional glimmers of strict Dad were a difficult, jagged pill to swallow. He could re-emerge when I least expected it. This version of him brought out my fiery anger and my full willingness to fight. When I was younger living in *my dad's house*, he had a way of taking the wind from my sails that went beyond deflating and left me questioning if I was even a boat. I'd often be cut off mid-sentence with, "When I'm talking, you listen!" or "You shut your mouth!" and the eventual "Stop your crying!" It wasn't so much the words that broke me down, but the severe, foreboding tone and look on his face that delivered the blows. Back then, my dad was a serious and intense man, but in the next moment, once the storm passed, he could be loving and kind. This behavior kept me confused and unsteady.

When I was in high school, Dad's encouragement for my future came in the form of concern around my choice to not take typing as an elective. If I had taken typing, he believed I would be able to get a job as a secretary when I graduated. I felt minimized by this. I wanted to go into advertising. I had been the president of the high school business club and had won first place in the area schools' advertising competition. I had been invited to compete in the North Atlantic Regionals in Florida. But it didn't matter--as a teenager, I had little say and felt like I counted for even less. As I grew older, my ideas have been met with his question, "What will X think about that?" X being the male in my life. It has felt as if I must always have a male qualifier before my ideas can be deemed valid.

In the years of my avoidance of my father, he did change. Maybe in retirement he finally had space in his life to let go. Once he retired, he and mom moved back south from Connecticut. Dad found his church, and he started to smile and laugh more. This was a version I had occasional faint memories of too. They were harder to get at but they were there.

My dad loved me—I knew that. I have never called myself a religious person, but I was comforted by my father's concern and promises of prayers and his rallying of the support of his church. This was his way of extending his love and support.

My mom's support was more difficult for me. Those we need the most, we can feel hurt by the most—and so shutting my mom out had been my default for a while.

My mom and I were the best when I was really young. I remember being six years old in the summer before school had begun, sitting with my mother on the front steps of our house.

"You're special," my mother said.

"I am?" I asked.

"We picked you. I wanted a girl more than anything in the world."

"And that's why you adopted me all the way from Korea," I said. I did feel special then. I knew the story and had heard it before, but I still loved it.

When I was a little girl, I could not get enough of my mom. Nothing was more exciting than waking up in the morning to discover my mom sleeping next to me. From time to time, my mom would quietly snuggle into my double canopy bed and join me as I slept. Back in those days, one of my favorite things to do was to pull out her old teen beauty pageant photographs. I would spend hours looking at my mom in awe as she stood on stage in her gown, tiara, and sash. My mother had been vibrant and beautiful.

I was the only girl of four children. And while I was potentially special, I understood it was amazing that I had been adopted, not that I was amazing. I soon found it could feel lonely and isolating, especially since I didn't look like my family or anyone else I knew for that matter. I was Korean and my family and community were all white. It was a strange feeling growing up in New Hampshire, where *Korean* was just another way to say, *Chinese*. I hated being Asian, or Oriental, as they all said back then.

When I was in the fifth grade, we moved from New Hampshire to Connecticut. I learned quickly there were many ways in which Connecticut was different from New Hampshire. For one, the girls went shopping for school clothes more than once a year. They bought new spring clothes, too. I had not heard of this before! I remember the day Abby Addison from across the street called me on the telephone and invited me over to see her new spring clothes. I had no idea what she meant by spring clothes, but I put on my sneakers and curiously made my way across the street.

Mrs. Addison and I sat at her kitchen table drinking Pepsi. The Addison's always offered Pepsi to their guests. Mr. Addison was a VP at Pepsi, and the way I understood it, VPs and their families had to drink Pepsi. Good thing I liked Pepsi and I was excited to see the spring clothes. Abby paraded into the kitchen wearing some of the prettiest, most fashionable outfits I had ever seen. She donned an array of blouses in light pinks, soft blues, and whites. However, I was mostly struck by the pinstripe pants and acid-washed jeans, which were just coming into style and she had both. Abby even had new shoes. I was so envious!

"Isn't she so pretty?" Mrs. Addison continued to ask as Abby fashioned each of her stylish outfits.

"Yes," was all I could say in between my fizzing gulps of Pepsi.

"When are you going shopping for your spring clothes?" Abby finally asked.

"Probably soon," I lied. I knew I would not be going spring clothes shopping. I had overheard my parents talking about the "spoiled kids around here" and something in my gut told me this was one of those things. I would have loved to fit in in this way, to have stylish new clothes for the season. But this social offense would be easier to navigate than what I had endured in New Hampshire, the problem being with my face.

The kids here didn't make fun of me for being Korean. This was even more odd than the spring clothes. In New Hampshire, I dreaded the school bus where the big kids were especially mean. They pulled at the edges of their perfectly round eyes, imitating mine while faking Chinese talk. "Ching-Chong," they'd say to me in laughter. This is when I learned that Korean was not just different but awful. I started to secretly wish on every birthday to be white. Being and feeling different back then was who I was every day, everywhere. I didn't fit in; I didn't belong anywhere. I wasn't unique like some magical unicorn—I stuck out like a sore thumb and got made fun of. My older brother Gabe emerged as my protector; he would always stick up for me. At home, he would still be the typical, antagonizing brother, but on the bus, he was my protective big brother. Connecticut didn't have the same hang up with my Asian-ness, but I didn't' give up the desire to be white because all the white girls were pretty and popular.

The summer before sixth grade, I recall staying up late watching movies on cable TV with my mom long after my dad had gone to bed. I loved this time alone with her; she was all mine— even my brothers had gone to bed. This had been a small window in time, where I remember us being "us."

Eventually, over the years, cut by cut, I disappointed my mother. I dropped out of cheerleading. I had tried out and made the team, thinking it would make her proud of me. She had been a cheerleader and had loved to reminisce about those days. But I was not as good as she had been. "Cheering today is not like it was in my day. The girls today are ridiculous," she said, but what I heard was, *I was ridiculous*. Then, there was the too much makeup. I could never get it right because of my eyes. "You don't want to look like a tramp," my mom would admonish. I heard, *You look like a tramp*. Once I mis-spelled horses on a mixed tape to say "hores" and she assumed I was listening to a song called "Bring on the Dancing Whores."

"What kind of sick music are you listening to? What are we supposed to think?" my mom yelled at me in disgust. I heard, *You are a sick person.* Being referred to as a tramp by my mom in my mind was just another term for *slut*. My mother's good southern Christian up-bringing would never have allowed her to have used the word *slut*, but my insecure and fractured teenaged self knew what she meant.

Both of my parents accused me of always talking back. I wanted to scream and yell and jump out of my body. They had no idea I was so angry. A gnawing feeling had begun to trouble me and keep me second guessing everything about myself. Then the bedroom raids of my journal began, mostly when I was away at friends' houses for sleepovers. Coming home the next morning was such an excruciating event that the stress would consume me. I knew that once I walked through the door, I would be met by my mom beckoning me to come to the family room where she and my father would be waiting with my journal in hand. I had tried so hard to hide the damn thing. It never occurred to me that I should have brought it with me when I left for the sleepover. My mom would ask me what was wrong with me. I had written about boy crushes and about being mad at my parents. They tried to make me read out loud to them what I wrote, but I had refused.

Our cycle of fighting would lead to months of dead silence. Most of the time my words got me in trouble. And when I carried on about wanting a career someday, my mother would say, "You think you are better than me." I didn't; I just wanted to go to college and have a career. I am certain I said some shitty things to my mom, so her interpretation of my words would have been a good read on the anger I was feeling back then.

Ultimately, I moved out and financed my education—this left a terrible scar on the relationship I had with both my parents for years. I understood this as me not being as valued as my brothers who I believed were always afforded more leniency and opportunity than me. Despite my relationship with my mom, I had wanted her to finally fight for me, to make my dad pay for my education like he was for my brother at the University of Southern California. In the end, I believed my mom just didn't like me.

The nature of our arguing changed a bit over time but the die had been cast. Mom and I triggered each other and heard each other's intentions with a certain hurtful filter. I was done with being hurt, and so over the years, I retreated further away.

***

"I feel so sorry for you," my mom said again and again.

I knew she meant that she was sad for me. But these words were difficult to hear. *Don't pity me*, was all I could think. The very thought I could be viewed as a "poor little girl" or as a helpless victim always triggered my inner tough girl, which was usually served with a side of anger. I would inhale, hold my breath, and let it out slowly. *Give her a break. This is not how she means it*, I tried to reason, but I rarely let my mom off the hook and it would be hard to start now.

"We'll be fine," I always said to her. I had no idea if we would be, but I'd die trying to make it so. I suspected my mom waited patiently on the sidelines for me to give any indication of my needing her. I wished I could let my mom love me in the way she knew how to, but it always left me feeling like I had to be someone else for it to work. Someone I didn't know how to be, and so I came up short.

***

The responsibilities of my life now and the baggage of my childhood were feeling heavy. One moment rolled into the next, and it was exhausting. Wyatt's therapist and school had been notified of our situation at home. I directed them not to tell Wyatt about Jeff's cancer. The ABA therapists were on standby with social stories about being sick to support Jeff's chemo sessions; nobody knew what to expect. None of my friends knew what to do to help, so they stayed on the periphery like planes waiting for the *okay* to enter my airspace and land next to me. Ashley had been my first call, later Paige, and then a couple of my other childhood friends, but no one else. I could not share this news because putting words to my feelings threatened the emotional fortifications I was constantly constructing and repairing.

It took a few days and a lot courage before I called Paige. She had lost her husband three years before when an aneurysm hit his heart. I felt selfish telling her. I kept putting off the call because I didn't want to suck her back into the vortex of fear and death of a spouse, but I knew she would know I needed her support. I sat on the sofa in my apartment after Wyatt had been put to bed and reached for my phone. I looked at my *Favorites* and found Paige's name and profile picture; it was of us hugging at my wedding. I pressed her name and the line rang a couple of times.

"Hello!" Paige said.

"Hi . . . um," I stalled, my voice already cracking. These calls were killing me. They were so hard. I always faltered, the words freezing before they could get out of my mouth.

"Meliss . . . what is it? What's wrong?" she asked, instantly changing the tone of her voice.

"Jeff is sick," I said.

I told her everything. I cried with Paige in the way my whole heart needed to. I didn't have to voice one single fear. She said each one for me, as I sobbed through, responding, "Yes, yes, and exactly." She knew. When a friend holds your heart like it's their own, it's not just connection, but love. We both cried and she reminded me that this was still the "good" cancer. She may have been one of the few people able to talk me back to the shallow end of the pool. By the time we hung up, I had rung out some of my sadness.

Caroline, Wyatt's nanny, had continued to come throughout the week as if it were a regular work week for me, but it wasn't. Caroline had started with us earlier that year when I went back to work. I had texted her Sunday evening, sharing the details of what had enfolded. I would not be able to talk with her in front of Wyatt when she arrived at the apartment. Caroline came and, without a sideways glance, got Wyatt ready for school. She didn't miss a beat and kept up the guise of normal. She was amazing. It was only Tuesday and already this felt like a routine I had been in forever. Once they left and the apartment was quiet, I could take a shower and get myself together and head to the hospital.

In the shower, the hot water warmed me and created a thin veil of steam to hide behind. This had become my cry confessional. The shower was the place I allowed myself to be sad and let all the *what ifs* run wild in my head. This was my place where fear and I sparred, and I usually lost. If Jeff had stage four cancer how many years would we have? What would those years look like? What would we be able to do? What would be important to do?

When I was done exhausting myself with the bullshit *what ifs*, I turned off the water, dried off, and got dressed. The face I saw in the mirror wasn't my own. It was a version of me that looked vacant, puffier, and uglier.

When I finally left my apartment, it was gray outside. Late March was the space between winter and real spring. It was ugly, raw, and forgettable; this was how I felt, too. I could see my car out the front door of the building, and as I approached my SUV, I noticed the resident wild turkey was sitting on top of it. Who the hell knew they could jump that high or fly?

This wild turkey had been living in the apartment parking lot for about a month. It was giant. No one could do anything about it and it just hung around, walking about, and everyone avoiding it because if you did get too close, it would emit an ugly loud squawk. And everyone knew wild turkeys were mean. It had tried to peck a few people who had gotten too close.

I stopped about fifteen feet from my car. I didn't want to approach. The last thing I needed was to get bitten by a turkey. I had nothing to shoo it off with. I looked around the parking lot for a giant stick, but there was nothing. So I reached inside my purse, grabbed my keys, and pressed the red alarm button on my key fob. The sound of the alarm *literally* scared the shit out of the wild turkey. He squawked and left a giant mess of bird poop--as if someone had wiped a soiled infant diaper down the driver's window and onto the handle. But it did the job and the wild turkey jumped off my car and took off through the parking lot. I stood there staring for a moment in disbelief. I had to crawl into the driver's seat through the passenger side door to avoid the river of turkey shit. At the car wash, the young, twenty-something kid approached my window, but not too closely. I cracked the window cautiously hoping some of the mess had dried enough not to fall into my car. He had a look of surprise and concern on his face.

"A wild turkey," I said flatly.

As the car wash conveyor connected to my front wheels and pulled my SUV into the car wash, streams of suds poured down my windshield and driver's side window, washing away the bird defecation, the mess. If only it were that easy in life.

13| fall 2005

By thirty-three, I had a solid version of my tough-girl self that kept me protected. Paige and I used to joke about my ridiculous attitude of "strike first, strike hard." Yes, it was a *Karate Kid* reference. As much as Paige found this funny, I knew she felt for me and my struggle. I would cut off my nose to spite my face if it meant I was protected from a bigger hurt. *You judged me? Well, I judged you more!* Jeff made life different for me, and I became less guarded with him. Over time, his calm, self-assured demeanor gained him access to behind-the-scenes of my tough-girl show. I found myself more willing to be messy and to admit fear as well as defeat with him. It didn't happen all the time, but more with him than with most.

I learned to armor up at an early age and practiced it throughout my teenage years. One of my earliest memories of realizing that I could control how hurt I felt was when I was in junior high. My parents and I had had a fight--maybe my mom had rummaged in my bedroom and read my journal again. Mostly, what I remember is sitting alone in my room on the green wall-to-wall carpet, against my bed, hiding from the world, writing furiously in my journal. I recall feeling ripped apart at my core and being furious with myself for crying so hard that my head actually hurt. I can still recall the hurt and loneliness from that night. Out of nowhere, I said out loud and then wrote, "I hate them." I didn't really, but in that moment, I felt abandoned, hateful, and mad. Indulging in this numbing emotion was like taking help from the wrong person. I knew saying the word *hate* was wrong, it even felt awkward, but it magically sealed up the sad, hurt parts of me. As I grew older, I repeated this trick again and again; when I felt hurt or fearful, I would turn my hurt into anger. Over time, the awkward, wrong feeling moved to the back of my heart and became the lesser of my voices guiding me. I decided that acknowledging feeling sad was a waste of time and only made me feel weak and pathetic.

Jeff's calm, however, grounded me. I breathed with him and in those breaths, I found it less necessary to push the sadness and hurt away. I rarely felt sad and when I did, he never judged or tried to change me. It was as if I could do an emotional trust fall with him and he would always catch me and ask if I was okay.

In the months leading up to our engagement, I was overcome with anxiety and self-doubt. I had to confess to Jeff some missteps I'd taken in my life so he could decide if he really wanted to be with me. I was so embarrassed by what I needed to say. My shame fell on me like a heavy, itchy sweater, and I needed to get it off of me. One night after work, I sat on Jeff's sofa. "I have something I have to tell you." My heart was racing. I could see the worry in his eyes. I wanted to say, *Don't worry, it's not that bad*, but it was. It was time to let him know what kind of person I had been.

On the surface, I was like most thirty-three-year-old women; I enjoyed my car, clothes, trendy cell phones, girl trips, Saturday nights out, and brunch. I was finally making a decent salary again and starting to save a little money. But there was another layer, just below the surface, that contained my backstory and my penance, which I carried with me because of a series of bad decisions and poor planning. "I have no money and I have very little savings," I blurted out. I continued because I couldn't stop now. If I stopped, some of the truth might get left behind like a solo sock in the dryer never to be found. "I am four years into bankruptcy. I have my finances under control now, but no big nest egg to join up with yours if we get married." I finished and looked past him out the windows into the night. I couldn't look him in the eyes, afraid of what I might see.

I knew now it was a big "if" we got married. The bomb had been dropped. It was finally out in the open. Would he break up with me? Would it be sudden or would he fade away over time? Standing emotionally naked before him made me nauseous, but it had to be done. I still couldn't believe I put myself in this position financially and now I was potentially putting him in the middle of my mess. I had never imagined I would want to marry and therefore this tidbit about my life never had to be exposed.

Two years of unemployment in the post-dotcom era had done a number on my bank account. Up until that point and even for a while after, I had felt invisible; I acted and spent irresponsibly. It took becoming flat broke for me to wake up and grow up. Jeff would think I was a fraud, and how could I blame him? Who I was now and who I had been were very different. He only knew the girl who had finally cut the shit and grown up.

Jeff held my gaze for a few seconds that felt like forever. Finally, he asked, "Is that it?"

"Yes," I said, feeling a mix of shame and relief for having put it out on the table. At the same time, dread took over. Jeff was different than me; he had gone to Yale and didn't have student loans or any debt at all. Over the past year, I had come to understand we had experienced life very differently. I didn't know if he would be able to wrap his head around the zigzags of my life. Mine had been more of a balancing act; something between struggle and an old-fashioned hustle. I had financed my way through a second-rate university while always working two to three jobs. I had a sometimes-turbulent relationship with my parents. And I followed a career path based on money, not passion. Jeff's story read like this: hockey and prep schools, followed by Yale, the NHL-draft, and a career-ending injury. But he rebounded and worked himself into a successful career in finance, doing something he loved. Additionally, Jeff and all of his siblings had what seemed like an ideal relationship with each other and their parents.

I waited in the eternal silence of those few seconds.

The night before, I had laid awake in my bed wondering if I should give up and break up with him to run from this embarrassment. I was angry with myself for even falling in love with him. I replayed an old conversation in my head, my male friends going on and on about women who had debt or no money. They referred to these women as "liabilities." I had shrunk a little every time one of these conversations came up because I was one of those women. This conversation was further accented by an old childhood memory of my father taking my mother's credit cards from her. I didn't fully understand the implications at the time, but I saw the impact, and my mother's desperate and angry reaction. I saw how a man, a husband, had control over a wife. To my seven- or eight-year-old self, I observed that if you had no job and no money, you had no say.

As I grew older, I also grew to believe that if you had a job that paid less, then you were less. After a couple of unsuccessful serious relationships, I had decided marriage and money did not mix. But here I was: I wanted to spend the rest of my life with Jeff and I was ashamed of my bankruptcy. I knew it was a result of a huge lack of personal maturity and accountability.

Jeff broke the silence. "Okay. We can work with that." He was so matter-of-fact. It was the strangest thing because I had lost sleep for weeks over this. "I trust your judgment. You're doing much better than you give yourself credit for," he said with a gentle smile. Jeff's words were full of compassion. Did I even deserve him?

14| march 2016

The afternoon sun arrived, warming and brightening the hospital cafeteria, making it feel less institutional. I sat alone at a small table against a window. Jeff's parents had left and would be back later. Jeff was napping for now and I was glad. I had the feeling he had been keeping himself awake for the constant flow of visitors parading in. My beef vegetable soup stared at me like a dark puddle. It was a better choice than the Welch's fruit snacks I had been consuming at an alarming rate. Sitting by myself felt good because I needed time with my thoughts.

My mind went to my job. How could I return to work? I had informed my manager of what was going on by email as I hadn't had the strength for a conversation. The words were too difficult and I worried I'd start crying. As my dad had informed me at the age of twenty-three, I must never cry at work if I wanted anyone to respect me. I can't recall the exact details of the inciting event, but I had come home from my first real job post-college, in tears, explaining what a witch my supervisor was. My mom asked what had happened with compassion and curiosity. She was on my side. My dad had stated simply, "You never cry at work." In the many years that followed, I had adhered to this rule, mostly. But, somehow, the last few years had snuck up and kicked my ass in the most surprising and personal ways: motherhood and now Jeff's cancer. I had put both Jeff and Wyatt at the core of my joy but events of their lives had also brought me to my knees with fear, insecurity, and tears.

I had asked that work keep my situation as quiet as was possible, notifying the immediate team only, and to let people know I didn't want to talk about it. I was offered as much time away as I needed.

How much time did I need? I couldn't think what a week would look like, let alone *weeks*. I wasn't sure I knew how to go back to work or even *how* to work anymore. Everything had changed. Every part of me wanted to say that I was never coming back.

Only a couple of months ago, I had been giddy with excitement to be back in the workforce again. I was thrilled that John, an old boss and mentor from a previous firm, wanted me on his team again. John was the chief technology officer at the firm, so he wouldn't have hired me if I were a complete idiot. I always found it hard to believe that I was as good as everyone else talked about me being. I knew I tried harder than most and could go toe-to-toe with anyone when it came to committing. Outwardly, I put on a confident face, but it always took a bit of an internal psych-up for me to get there.

I was now haunted by the idea that my capability--or lack thereof--would be footnoted as the woman whose husband has cancer. My mistakes might be chalked up as me being distracted-- "You know her husband is sick"--or maybe it would be said, "Wow, despite the sad situation at home, she's doing great." Even worse, people would want to share their cancer stories with me. I didn't want to be in the pool of those people who wore their colors of support. I wanted to be average and without exceptions.

When Wyatt had been diagnosed with autism, I had shared selectively at first and eventually openly at work, as my schedule increasingly took on modifications for hosts of appointments. Colleagues loved to share their stories of friends or distant family members or even neighbors who were on the spectrum. They loved to send links to resources for me to read or book suggestions. I hated everyone's opinions and sharing. This one was always fun: "My neighbor is autistic. He's great. We just love him." What did that mean? Were you expected not to like him? They always asked, *How's Wyatt doing?* when I would arrive late from an appointment. *Still autistic,* I wanted to say. I was angry at the time. My plan for my life had blown up, and I believed everyone was treating me with pitying kindness.

And here I was again.

Jeff had made the promise that he would not die before me. Years ago, I had gone to see the movie *P.S. I Love You* with my friend Karishma, and while it was an endearing movie, it nauseated me. My fear had always been of Jeff dying before me. I told myself I could not survive that. When I thought of being left alone and abandoned my heart and head spun. On several occasions, I told Jeff that if anything happened to him they would find me in a corner and have to peel me off the floor. After *P.S. I Love You,* I came home and told Jeff how upset I was by the thought of him dying first. He made light of it. "Not going to happen," he said. "We'll die together. Deal?"

15| march 2016

On Wednesday, when I arrived at the hospital, the door to Jeff's room was open. I could hear his parents inside as I approached. The blue vinyl chair next to Jeff's hospital bed was empty, waiting for me. My spot. The chair had the illusion of comfort, but after about thirty minutes, the cheap foam padding reminded me that my left hip and low back were over age forty. Jeff's mom and dad would assume one of the other chairs or stand; they knew sitting too long was a bad idea. I should have followed their lead.

A small knock came from the door and Dr. Cornbloom appeared.

"Hello, Blaesers," she said, and then directed her attention to Jeff. "Jeff, how are you feeling today?"

"Good," Jeff said. He always said good.

"I have good news," she said. "The labs are in and I'm happy to tell you your margins were all clean and the results are showing Stage Two B." I had no idea what "B" meant, but I inhaled deeply and sighed with an indescribable relief. It was as if someone had rolled back the clock and given us years of our life back together. Dr. Cornbloom explained that Jeff's staging was rare and complicated. The tumor had breached the abdominal wall and it had perforated during the biopsy, essentially releasing microscopic cancer cells into Jeff's abdomen and potentially blood stream. The concern and risks were that the cancer cells were microscopic, so it was important that chemo be the very next step to make sure all the cancer was attacked in case it had traveled. They had prepared for this outcome, which was why he had the colostomy bag. Jeff would be able to start chemo in a month. This was sooner than if he had not had the colostomy bag. After chemo, more testing would be done to ensure there was no spreading and that nothing new had developed. The good news was his lymph nodes were clean. This was one of the key details that kept Jeff's cancer from being at a higher stage. The technicalities that defined staging were above my pay grade, but I listened as best as I could to this foreign language.

I was uncomfortable with risk, so I always looked to be prepared for it. I still heard the caution in the good news and the possibility that this nightmare might not be over. I imagined the breaking of the tumor spreading like the reenactments of a sneeze with its millions of germ particles scattering. There was a plan, though, and I would cling to that. I could get my head around this. I smiled, hiding my concern. I didn't want everyone to know just how scared I had been or that I was still scared.

"Yes!" Sylvie erupted.

Joe was smiling with his mouth, but his eyes wore the real smile of relief; his son was going to be okay. Their joy lifted me.

16| march 2016

Six months of chemotherapy was ordered.

"We are a team," I told Jeff. I would obviously be at every treatment with him. "Where you go, I go." This was a long-standing saying we always repeated to each other when making plans when the other's attendance seemed optional.

I had arranged with my manager that my already-abridged work schedule would now be even more abridged. I would work four days a week, leave early twice a week on Wyatt's ABA therapy days, and work remotely on Jeff's chemotherapy days, every other week. Additionally, I would be out for ad hoc doctor appointments two to three times a month. It wasn't too long before the guilt set in like a dark rain cloud. Did I have the right to ask for this much? I was making my problems everyone else's problems. Didn't I despise people like me? How would my projects stay on track? I couldn't shake these thoughts.

Brandon, my manager, had given me his full attention as I sat across from him explaining my need to be with Jeff during chemo. He was unwavering.

"Of course. Take whatever time you need. We support you," he had said and seemed genuine. I wasn't sure if I was uncomfortable with the ease and graciousness of his care or the situation I was in, but taking kindness and help always felt borrowed.

"Thank you," I managed, but felt like I needed to say something more.

The firm hired a contractor and extended a consulting firm we had been working with already to fill in the gaps, but that wasn't in the annual budget; no one had to tell me that. I knew all about creating and managing budgets and overhead. It had been a big part of my life at my previous job.

I wondered if I should quit and let them move on, but the selfish part of me became acutely aware that I needed to work. Three weeks ago, I thought I would not be able to walk back into the office. But now, I needed to be in a space where I could be me. My colleagues were holding up their end of the bargain and everyone was respectful of my personal situation in the same quiet way no one talked about Fight Club. For a few hours a day at work, I was not the wife of the man with cancer or the special needs mom. Each of the labels I wore and the roles I played had started to claim parts of me, but at work, in my quiet little office, I could cocoon myself away from the world and the realities of my life.

17| may 2016

A month into chemo, Jeff looked tired. I could see the hollowing under his eyes and the thinning of his hair. He had lost a significant amount of weight since his stay in the hospital and now chemo was starting to take its toll, too.

The radiology center was not what I expected. There was just a bit more privacy between chairs than I anticipated, but not much. The patient chairs reminded me of souped-up recliners, but like all medical facilities, it was cold and sterile. Jeff's nurse had given him a warm blanket to keep him from feeling chilled. I had planned on the cold and was bundled in a fleece jacket. Again, we were the youngest people in the room, minus the support person. Everyone looked at us with curiosity. I brought my laptop with me with the intention of doing work. At a minimum, I thought I'd check email, but I couldn't do it. This was an awful place and I wanted to be fully connected in each moment with Jeff.

"Have you heard from the builder?" Jeff asked.

"What do you think?" I asked.

"I'll take that as a *no*." He smiled and I laughed a little. The *I'll take that as a* phrase was something Wyatt had started saying when he thought there was too long a pause after he asked a question. "Mommy, can I have a strawberry popsicle?" he would ask at 7:00 a.m. If I paused, looking for the right words, other than a flat *no*, the pause would quickly be filled with, "I'll take that as a *yes*." I sometimes wondered if I let Wyatt get away with too much--what my grandmother would have called--fresh talk. I wanted my son to have a voice and speak his mind, but I also wanted him to have respect.

The layer of complexity that autism piled on Wyatt often left me questioning myself as a parent. I knowingly moved the line of *okay* and *not okay* depending on the situation, but to an outsider, it could look inconsistent and nonsensical. We had been waiting on the house completion date for over a year. And when I say date, I mean *target month*. Building this house was one of my worst decisions, even worse than when I proclaimed that Jeff and I would go to the Grand Opening of Ikea years ago. Getting to Ikea on that fateful day was evidence of what a tolerant man Jeff was. I had uprooted him on a rainy, cozy day watching football, because I was bored, to sit on the side of the highway waiting to exit and then sit in more local traffic for three hours. The whole time, he was patient, even funny, and he never even suggested that we turn around. In the end, we left Ikea with shitty frozen meatballs that were eventually tossed.

I doubted that we'd "toss" the house--we were in this until the bitter end. The builder blamed everything and everyone but his inability to return a phone call or text. I wasn't really clear on whose fault that was. I never would have predicted our previous house would have sold so fast and that we would be living in an apartment complex with a mean wild turkey who shat on cars. Or that Jeff would get cancer. None of this was in my life's project plan or even listed as a risk. So, I guessed, sure, maybe our builder had some unforeseen circumstances in his plan, too. Who knew? Or cared.

At this juncture, I should have known my life was not going according to the plan. I went from *I'm not getting married* to *I want to marry Jeff! Let's never leave Boston* to *Jeff, we should buy a house. I can't imagine having kids* to *Jeff, what do you think about having a baby, like within the next year?*

When Jeff was first diagnosed with cancer, his parents suggested that we get out of the house project and move in with them. For a flash of a moment, it was as inviting as a breath of fresh air. This "get out of jail free" card felt like the clouds parting and the heavens talking to me, but the voice in my head reminded me that this would be giving up. I hated the feeling of losing and letting life beat me. And so, not letting all those years of good training on how to "stand your ground and commit" go to waste, I imagined the relief for only a moment and then let it go. Whether it was a good or bad choice, it was undoubtedly the one that meant taking help and that never came easily to me. What did come easily was what I had learned from my mom: she always had the power and sheer will to stand her ground, unmovable, much like I'd imagine Queen Elizabeth had among the men of her time.

The house and the builder were speed bumps in my life, ones that I had opened the door to. We didn't need to build a new home. We didn't even need to move. So many decisions were being laid at my feet, things that should have been fun, but, instead, I covered them in a thick layer of guilt, smothering every drop of potential enjoyment. Choosing lighting and bathroom fixtures, flooring, countertops, and fighting the builder over custom window sizes, made me feel like a grossly materialistic person. I hated people like that. The idea to build to bring us together wasn't working. Life had changed and the house wasn't important anymore, but the money committed by this point weighed on me. This was not the kind of money you walked away from. *Let it go, this is bullshit you don't really care about*, I would tell myself. The other part of me, the version who planned projects and managed budgets, saw these as tasks and details that needed to be done according to signed contracts and plans. I was irate by what felt like a lack of professionalism. I just needed it to be over, and I didn't like to lose.

The beeper sounded on the small white monitor: the first part of treatment was done. It was time for part two. This second part of the chemo treatment would be administered over the next two days. Jeff would take the chemo with him. He had had a port surgically installed into his chest where a catheter would be attached to deliver the treatment to him. Jeff would wear a fanny pack around his waist that carried the reservoir of chemo. A battery pack powered the pump, which pushed the chemo into his body. This was the new routine. Jeff never complained; he always did what was needed. I imagined what he must have been like as an athlete in training. One more skating drill, all focus and action, no complaining. I was starting to see our likeness in a light I hadn't before. We didn't complain when it might show weakness.

I waited for Jeff in the lobby as he made an appointment for the next round of blood work. Behind the reception desk was an oversized painting that, normally, I would have said was beautiful. Actually, the first time I saw it, I did think that, but over time, I saw it as ironically annoying. On a dark gray, stormy sky, beautiful vibrant yellow flowers stood in the foreground. The clumpy texture of the yellow paint gave life to the flowers in a way that gave them strength. I supposed the idea was a symbol: the storm the patients were weathering and the vibrant yellow of the flowers their life, but lately, I was bitter, so screw the painting.

***

It was late May, IEP time was here, according to the official invitation to a planning meeting from the school. Sue, Wyatt's advocate, made the process easier than it had been in previous years, but it was still an enormous amount of work, both intellectually, but more so emotionally. IEP time felt heavy and like a "make-or-break time" every year. I knew one year's plan was not going to be the plan that unlocked all the brilliance I saw inside my son, but it always felt that way. And, year after year, I was the one who signed off on the plan. I reviewed and approved the goals that were meant to bring Wyatt success. Every year, I wandered into a territory where I was the only participant who did not have an advanced degree in special education, yet I was expected to know what to ask for and to approve this document for his success. I was Wyatt's mother, and I would not have anyone else responsible for him, however, the constant negotiating and posturing of IEP-planning time could be soul-crushing, intimidating, and triggered every insecurity I had about myself. Was I smart enough? Was I a good enough mother to get this right? I wanted everyone to want his success in the way I wanted his success, but I needed more help. I felt so alone as I poured over nine-point font, single-spaced documents provided by the school that made my eyes cross. Didn't these twenty-six-year-old teachers know this was too damn small to read?

When I first learned Wyatt's autism qualified him for an IEP, I thought, *my son is special; they care*! It was like a little piece of magic. I was amazed until the reality set in. The magic only happened for the best negotiators and the most prepared. Year after year, I prepared frantically, lining up all of Wyatt's materials, including neuropsych reports, external evaluations from speech and OT, the previous year's progress reports, and state academic standards, etc. Jeff and I would show up for the disappointing process and we would always wonder if the administrative team had taken training in talk-torture. Jeff and I had assumed our parenting roles with little to no discussion when Wyatt was born, and then they were further cemented when we learned of his autism diagnosis. I was the planner and Jeff, the supporter.

During the course of the meetings, my mind would go to billable hours, a carry-over from my consulting days. The caliber of these meetings would have never been acceptable and there would have been some serious feedback for someone. The conversation was often like a meandering river; it had no care for time and little use of an agenda. I was amused when the special education coordinator would roll her eyes at her colleagues as an indication that she believed they were going off track. I was unaware of this tactic as an effective meeting facilitation style.

The result of the planning meeting was always the same: an IEP that was ambiguous with just enough specificity to cover their asses and make you think the goals were reasonable. This year, my appetite for disappointment was being sated by everything and everyone, so I was annoyed before we even got to the meeting. My inner perfectionist hated the discomfort of the imperfect IEP. The special education coordinator dashed into the meeting late, sunglasses on top of her head, took a seat, and announced the meeting would need a hard stop at 1:30 p.m.

What if I grabbed her sunglasses and threw them against the wall--what would people do? That would be a hard stop.

"Sure," I agreed, "fine with us." But I was wrong--the IEP turned out to be satisfying for once! After almost two years of various tests, meetings, and me losing my shit on anyone who would listen, the school agreed with the neuropsychologist's evaluation and a consult from an outside reading specialist that Wyatt did have a reading disability. Wyatt needed a special reading curriculum and it needed to be taught to him by a reading specialist. Winging it would no longer fly. The school was onboard and this was a small ray of light. My baby would emerge.

Other small victories included finding a food delivery service, Sun Basket. My mind could not handle the simple task of planning out and shopping for healthy meals that actually tasted good. I worried about this all the time. Whatever Jeff was putting into his body had to be healthy. Sun Basket deliveries were a welcome sight in the refrigerator. Caroline would unpack everything neatly, and I was grateful for this luxury. Most nights during the twenty-minutes-or-less meal prep, my mind thought about work and all the things I hadn't been able to complete or didn't feel on top of. I couldn't stop thinking about and noticing where colleagues were being put into positions to cover my shortcomings, including my boss. I noticed he was updating our confluence project space with project statuses to cover for me, too. Initially, returning to work was a haven, but now my quiet walk down the office hall in the early mornings was like a corporate walk of shame. Dread would seep into my brain and pollute my thinking and cover me from head to toe. *The slacker has arrived,* heralded my inner voice.

***

Jeff's forty-seventh birthday was a nice break. I had arranged a dinner with fifteen of Jeff's friends, couples we knew and he had been close with for years. Typically, Jeff was never the type to celebrate anything, but I wanted him to be with friends and feel their love. Even if he was not one to lament his emotions, I could not believe that anyone could go through as much as he had and not want to be in the company of friends who knew and loved you since childhood. The evening was perfect. The restaurant had given us a private area and prepared a special menu for our group. The night was easy and I watched Jeff smile and laugh as his friends swapped stories and poked fun at each other. I wanted to bring joy to Jeff for his birthday and his friends helped me do this. Jeff's genuine laughter had been missing for so long, it made me happy to experience it again. Jeff was what I called a quiet smiler--his smiles were small, or at least they had been with me lately.

At home, as the weeks wore on, there was little space for Jeff to escape my gaze. I didn't know how he was feeling day-to-day, except for what I could see. I also wondered when he would see me again, know that wherever he was in his mind, I was there too, waiting for him to invite me in. Jeff moved somewhat cautiously around me. He never asked for help and he never talked to me about what was going on. It was as if we had just experienced a "smash and grab" from a robber who had come into our life, smashed up what we knew, scared the crap out of us, and left us huddling in fear. And in the robbery, they took what was left of our connection. I knew in my heart he loved me, or at least I kept telling myself this, but I wondered why he kept stepping around me.

In hindsight, I see now we were just where we had been before the cancer had arrived, but his illness had added a complexity to our growing distance. We had been on separate sides of the room for a while and then brought together only briefly by a scary moment. In our moment of *holy shit* there was no question how much we loved each other, but now, he was retreating into himself again with more on his mind. I was being shut out again, but this time, I was more afraid than ever before.

18| june 2016

Our marriage counselor's office was another lackluster waiting room. Someday, I thought, I'm going to own a business, any business, and the waiting area is going to be like a spa. I stared at the brown-paneled walls. They reminded me of the basement in the house I grew up in Connecticut. I hated that basement; it may have had something to do with the fact that the previous owner's teenage son had painted on the back wall a skeleton with an ax that looked to be coming through a hole in the wall with the words "Helter Skelter" written below it. The nightmare-inducing mural had been painted over as soon as we moved in and later, wood-paneled over, but it was unforgettable to my twelve-year-old mind.

This waiting room had nothing eerie about it, just bad décor. I sank into the sofa--I would need a hand getting to my feet. Jeff, sitting in the straight-backed chair across from me, had made the better choice.

Jeff found Lynn, our counselor, online. I read her biography; she seemed nice, that is to say, her picture looked warm and approachable, but as soon as I saw the waiting area, I thought maybe I would have picked someone else. No, that wasn't really true. I was letting distractions become priorities, which usually happened when things were spinning out of my control. Jeff and I agreed that a cancer support group was not for us. We were not the support group type. The closest thing to a support group I had experienced was Wyatt's Early Intervention Parents group. Mostly, I felt like a voyeur in those meetings to other people's problems, wondering in what ways I was similar or different. A cancer group might support us on some level, but I wondered if we needed to go deeper and first address some foundational work, which would be better suited for a closed session. The tension in our marriage had started before Jeff got sick; this was not hard for us to acknowledge, or not for me anyway.

"I'm unhappy," I had said to Jeff one day. It had taken me awhile to actually allow the words to exit my mouth, but the feeling had taken root in me and I had hoped that saying the words would stunt their growth. I was conflicted by the timing of my announcement; only a "selfish wife" would do this. Jeff had only recently started chemo. But holding it in could be worse--I might explode.

"I know. What can I do to help?" Jeff asked kindly. He wasn't angry or put off. It was as if he had known for a while, too, but was waiting for me to be the one to say it.

He meant it; he wanted to help, but it pissed me off because I didn't want to tell him how to help me, I wanted him to just know. In my mind, I had already told him in various ways over the years. Repeating myself in that moment tasted bitter.

What really nagged and annoyed me was Jeff's relentless encouragement and support for me: my need to travel, the girl trips, going halfway around the world for work and leaving him with our son, and then me leaving my career. He supported my whim to get certified as a yoga teacher and supported me when I decided that teaching yoga wasn't for me. He always supported me during my family's fallings-out--he consistently saw my point of view and protectively sided with me. I was selfish and ungrateful. How could I ask him for more? And yet, I needed more. It sounded childish in my head, but when I thought about it, I just wanted to be included in what he was thinking and feeling. I missed being his best friend.

And then, sure and steady like the rise of a river, I was flooded with the realization that I was in debt to Jeff for my happiness, and that feeling was hollowing me out. The more I tried to remain grateful, the angrier I became. I carried my gratitude and need to level-up as my new bankruptcy.

But I was conflicted when I did an accounting of my life, so many issues had quietly crept up on me. For years I quarter-backed Wyatt's needs while trying to prove myself in my career and serve as cruise director for our marriage. And, in the daily details of our life I was staffing coordinator, interviewer, and trainer for babysitters, plus the general chief operating officer of our household. The only time I had for myself was on my yoga mat or in stolen moments on my drives to CVS.

I had already lost bits and pieces of myself *before* the arrival of The Cancer, and now, I was more overwhelmed than ever. I didn't know how to get back to Jeff and our life. My sense of gravity was gone. We used to complete each other's sentences and a shared glance could tell a story. Everyone used to seem just a little less interesting than us. Now, I was just lonely.

I did my best to explain my feelings to Lynn, the counselor. She took notes occasionally while giving smiles and nods. Jeff agreed with most things and answered a few of Lynn's questions with short yes-no responses. Verbose was not going to be an adjective for my husband in these sessions. At the end of the first session, Lynn happily summarized, "you obviously love each other very much!" *Gee, thanks,* my inner jerk said.

19| july 2006 – october 2007

In the beginning, our marriage was easy. It was like dating except we had a piece of paper that meant shared taxes and other legalities. We lived in the same condo. We ate at the same restaurants. We had the same routines. Jeff played golf. I biked and sometimes went to yoga. I hadn't even legally changed my last name.

Jeff started calling his condo "our" condo the moment we set my boxes inside the front door. I appreciated the gesture, but I needed to feel woven into our space beyond a trinket or two. I wanted to feel I was not a visitor in my own life but here to stay. "Visiting" is how I used to characterize times in my life when I knew I was passing through a phase that didn't really connect to who I was.

Gradually, we made small changes. The condo's cream-colored walls were painted a sage green with a Ralph Lauren red accent wall in the dining room, which, oddly, Max, my Siamese cat, meowed at incessantly. We also replaced the brown bachelor sectional with a cozy cream-colored sofa--not a couch but *sofa*. I loathed the old sectional. Jeff had never gotten or installed the hardware to keep the sections together and as a result, I consistently sat right in the middle of two sections that parted like the Dead Sea.

Back then, Jeff and I were focused on our careers. Jeff had landed a new job the day before our wedding. He was an analyst for a firm based in New York and would travel back and forth a good deal. I was slugging it out in the world of software consulting, trying desperately to establish my footing in a herd of--what I thought--were much smarter people than me. Software consulting in the financial world was a stretch for me.

Two years earlier, I had dove into the deep end of the pool without knowing how to swim when I joined the ranks in software consulting. Before that job, I had been in roles running projects for website design, but software implementation and this kind of financial subject matter was completely different than my dotcom days and my short stint at Fidelity working on mutual funds.

***

By the end of 2006, we had been married for six months, Jeff and I were headed to Costa Rica for "honeymoon number two," as I called it. We had planned to go to Costa Rica for our honeymoon right after we were married, but that had been Costa Rica's rainy season, so we opted for a trip to the Bahamas for "honeymoon number one." I had just kicked my first of what would be a streak of colds for the winter season and I was ready for a break. On top of that, my project at work had become a wild beast I could not get my arms around let alone tame.

We arrived in Costa Rica late at night. The resort, Tabacon, had sent a driver to pick us up in a white van with their logo stuck to its side, which was a good thing. The white van was one resort decal away from looking like a kidnapper van. Our driver spoke little English. He approached us, smiling, holding his sign with our name on it.

"Blah-zers?" he asked happily.

"Yes," Jeff said.

"Welcome, welcome. Come. *Vamanos*. We go," he said, as he loaded our bags into the conspicuous van.

Jeff and I were driven through hours of switchbacks that went further and further into the interior of the country in order to get to our resort. I held Jeff's hand as my other hand death-gripped the armrest. More than once our driver opted for unpaved roads littered with potholes and the occasional odd obstruction in the way. The pitch black night and overgrowth reached high enough over the roads to block the sky out in some areas making it difficult to see anything but the shadowy outlines of the forest. This natural eeriness contributed to my uneasy feeling which was only made worse by my growing nausea.

We arrived at Tabacon, a little car sick, but unscathed. Our driver shifted into tour guide mode and he directed us to look up. In the distance, we could see the faint glow of lava--Mt. Arenal was an active volcano.

"Wow, cool," I said, trying to be polite. I really didn't care at the moment. What I needed was sleep. Exiting the air-conditioned van as fast as I could, I was engulfed by a veil of humidity that settled on my skin. It felt like nature had sneezed all over me. The air had not only gotten notably thicker but more fragrant. We were in the rainforest. The heaviness of the night air only made me more tired. We entered our suite to find our bed had been made up with rose petals and origami swans made out of towels, but the romantic sentiment was lost to my exhaustion, and I passed out.

In the light of day, and my now rested disposition, Costa Rica was beautiful. Green and lush and with barely any cell service. I could not check my emails even if I wanted to--and I did not want to. Jeff, on the other hand, found a way to stay connected to work. He had a couple of calls to make, which he ultimately did by payphone on the side of the road just outside of the resort. He had year-end earnings to be concerned about. Jeff spoke a work language I was only topically tuned into. I envisioned Jeff surrounded by little coatimundis while on his calls. They looked like a cross between a raccoon and a meerkat. I noticed them milling about in packs every time we walked by the roadside phone booth.

I fell in love with the smells, sights, and sounds of Costa Rica's natural world. It demanded every bit of my senses and left no room for the typical noise that put me out of sorts. Our resort was at the base of Mt. Arenal, the active volcano pointed out the night before, which created hot springs--some with little waterfalls--all around the resort that guests could lounge in. We visited the hot springs every day. One day we ziplined through the treetops of the rainforest, and on another, we hiked and canoed.

I was amazed by the wildlife--sloths, birds, and even the very loud howler monkey who had taken residence in one of the nearby resort trees. In a place like this, who I was or who I felt like I was supposed to be didn't matter; the beauty was so overpowering, everything else paled in comparison. One afternoon, I indulged in a private yoga practice in an open pavilion set in the middle of the lush forest. I hadn't really developed a practice at this point in my life, but I was drawn to the quiet solitude and the idea of a reset. The air was thick and humid, and the surrounding hot springs splashed in chorus with the sounds of the nearby animals. I was entirely immersed. I found grounding within my body and a buoyancy in my mind with each pose. I had reset.

Returning from Costa Rica and falling back into the routine of life at home was fine, but the time away from work made my misfit feeling deepen with the sullen hue of doubt. Despite gradually finding my place at the firm, I was never one of the ones who had drunk the Kool-Aid.

While on most days I could find humor in the culture, I didn't always abide by the rules, like coming up with a team cheer for my project teams. Despite my discomfort, I did respect the culture deeply and I had grown to love the certainty of the structure. My truth, however, was this: I didn't love the work. The subject matter and clients were mentally, and sometimes emotionally, trying.

Not long after my return home from Costa Rica, I struggled with self-doubt and anxiety regularly. My "I'm not smart enough" demons continued to be bolstered by my cohort of heavily-pedigreed colleagues and clients. My insecurities were triggered like missiles for battle and the massive launch could not be called back this time. All-too-frequent software releases running into the small hours of the morning had me at my wit's end and I was exhausted. Every day I showed up in what I hoped was the most confident version of myself, starting with the outer layers--suit, careful makeup, humor and focus for my team, and a friendly, unflappable shell for my clients. But it was all an act, and I could feel it deteriorating. I'd open my email and the f-bombs would start coming out of my mouth as if I had Tourette's Syndrome.

The weekends should have provided a temporary refuge; the latest software release was done. Releases always stressed me out, so when they were over, I usually found some breathing room. But Jeff and I had started casually looking at houses, which added to my feeling of failure. I had come to terms with buying a house together meant the mortgage would be in Jeff's name only. I was still in my period of bankruptcy, and I was concerned with how the bank might view a joint credit application. I thought the least I could do was stay at this job, despite my growing anxiety, until we found a house. I had considered looking for another job but who knew how long it would take for me to find one. I needed to make money, my way to contribute and feel the same as Jeff. But I wasn't the same as Jeff. Everything was hard for me.

The following week, I was sitting at the kitchen island behind my laptop obsessing over another software release as Jeff rummaged through the cabinets, puzzling over dinner.

"I hate my job. I can't do it. I thought I could, but I can't," I said. It was out before I could stop it. We had been married less than a year, and I was already pulling the "I need to quit my job." Jeff stopped what he was doing, stood in front of me, and without a hint of emotion, he said. "So quit. I support whatever you want to do."

I wasn't prepared for this response. I thought he'd tell me *it'll get better* or *hang in there.*

"I don't have another job lined up," I said.

"You'll find one. Don't worry about it," said Jeff. I had been unemployed before, which had led to my financial downfall. Didn't he see what a bad idea this was? While I knew Jeff would never try to make me feel indebted to him, I remembered my mother's battle for independence and "her money." I took about a week to devise a plan. I decided I would start looking for a job immediately and see what I could line up for interviews and give my current job plenty of heads up that I was leaving. I appreciated the opportunity they had given me, but I also accepted I might have to be unemployed just to get out of this situation. I shared with Jeff the broad strokes of my plan, and, as always, he simply said, "I trust you. Do whatever you think is best for you."

In my mind, I made an agreement for the two of us. We would have to put buying a house on hold. I would slow things down until I knew I had something to contribute other than an opinion.

***

John--who had been my mentor and manager at the firm--and I were sitting in a small conference room at the client site. I stared past him out the glass door to the giant donut painting on the wall. Eye contact would be hard. I was indebted to him for taking me under his wing. I took a breath and spat it out.

"So, I've made a decision. After this next release, I have to leave." I had reasoned this was responsible and would serve both our needs. Departures mid-release were always painful to the project.

"Okay, when do think you'll you be back?" John asked.

I broke my gaze from the donut; I had not been clear enough. I had forgotten that in consulting people often took leaves as a way to "recharge" from projects and then came back.

"Oh, no wait, um, what I meant is that I'm leaving, leaving. It isn't working for me here," I explained.

"Oh, I see," said John, with a flicker of surprise.

"I'm sorry, it's me. I feel really bad," I said.

"Did something happen? Is it the client? I know the client can be challenging," said John. John and I were the same age, but for some reason, I always felt like his younger sister. It was hard to not be brutally honest about what a hot mess I felt like, but at the same time, despite our good working relationship, he was my boss.

"Yes and no, but not really," I said.

"I know the releases have been hard with them going so late, but I think they are going to even out soon," John said. I could tell he understood how hard things had been for me.

"It's not so much that. I just feel like the team would be better off with a more technical project manager. Carl helps me so much and I feel awful always leaning on him. I just can't do it anymore. I hate the feeling." I confessed my half-truth. Carl was the architect on the project, and I knew without him I'd have drowned months ago. He was a technical genius—I was not. The other half of my truth I'd keep buried. I felt in my heart I would always fall short. I would never be smart enough to learn all the technical pieces and financial subject matter.

John heard me out with patience. "Do you have another job lined up?" he asked. I wasn't ready for the kindness I heard in his voice. There was no accusation, the way some bosses and managers put you on the spot as if you had betrayed the firm by choosing to leave.

"No, I figured I'd start looking during the next couple of months while we plan the release. If I find something, great, if not, I'll just go home," I said.

John sat for a few quiet moments thinking. I wondered if this was the part when he would say, *Don't worry about the next release; you can leave now.*

"I might have something I think you would be good at, and it would really help me and Steve get the account in order, operationally." John and Steve had been building and running a large account over the past couple of years. I had no idea what account operations were and it wasn't lost on me that maybe John was just trying to help me out. I assumed this would likely not be a long-term thing, but it would give us all something we needed. Me, time to find something new, and in the meantime, I could help them as best as I could. I was intrigued mostly by John's confidence in me to do a good job. So, I didn't quit. My ego glowed and sang to me, *You're wanted!* I am sure he saw through my line of bullshit and insecurity, but, oddly, he still believed in me. I took the new, made-up role working for John and Steve at the company, initially running operations on the large Boston account. We would eventually call this work Business Operations, a new concept at the firm. Two years later, I would take John's idea, build it out, and execute it globally--this would become the Global Markets Business Operations Teams and the model for the entire organization. I began to see so many opportunities for improvement that ideas poured from me like water from a faucet.

I finally found a rhythm at work. I loved solving every problem that came my way. I discovered my sweet spot was problem-solving issues that involved business processes, technology, and people. I had partnered with a good many brilliant analysts who had sharpened my thinking when it came to dissecting a problem and my client management skills had prepared me to deal with even the most demanding internal colleagues.

Soon, I had two direct reports, and, while I was technically their manager, I rarely saw myself as their boss. We became partners in crime at work and my voice of self-doubt quieted to a low hum. I found ways to manage the spikes in volume by running, biking, taking the occasional yoga class, and traveling.

Jeff was also finding his sweet spot. Wall Street liked him as a top analyst in his space--toys. I had saved a copy of the *Wall Street Journal* listing Jeff's accomplishment. Jeff was modest and if he saw that I had done this, it would have probably made him uncomfortable, but I was proud of him. I loved his quiet and unassuming intelligence. Every now and again, Bloomberg TV would ask him to come in for a spot. It was fascinating for me to see him in this context. I banked all of his wins and quietly celebrated him, hoping his old firm was seeing his success. Jeff's last firm had laid him off, and while he never talked about it, I knew it was a bit of a blow. Jeff had never been good at office politics and it had cost him. But now, Jeff had come back with a *fuck you* by rising up. I could not have been happier for him.

I wondered what it was like to be Jeff, my loving and quietly confident husband. He never complained or needed validation like I did. I never saw in him "fight or flight" mode. Was it his time in sports? Was it his upbringing? As I considered our differences, over time, the question changed. It became less of a riddle and more of something I was glad for. I began to feel at ease with the differences in our historical context. Jeff had experienced life differently than me, but we were similar in the ways that mattered; commitments were binding, our word was a commitment, and we both knew what it meant to work hard for something.

Once again, I was sleeping soundly and breathing easier and I found myself excited again to be looking at houses on weekends. Everything felt easy, including work, and we melded into an "us" by joining our interests together through our support and encouragement for each other. Nothing in our lives was complicated. We focused on career goals, dinner plans with friends, vacations, and lazy afternoons. Well, sometimes dinner at home could get a little complicated.

Jeff and I shared dinner responsibilities. The nights Jeff cooked were always a bit more interesting--preparing a meal instead of ordering in or warming up food was new ground for him. One night, I called home and asked Jeff to start the chicken. It was easy: chicken breasts in a covered pot, stewed tomatoes, garlic cloves thrown in, then it all went in the oven, and I would finish the rest when I got home.

When I reached home, the faint smell of food met my nose. He had done it. Great. Dropping my bags and kicking off my shoes, I made my way into the kitchen.

"Thanks for starting dinner," I said, opening the oven and pulling out the pot. Inside the pot was the chicken, stewed tomatoes, and floating garlic skins. Where were the cloves? I poked around the pot.

"Jeff, what happened to the garlic cloves?" I asked.

"I put them in," he said, looking up from the news. Then it hit me. Jeff did not know the middle part was the good part. In those days, that was the magnitude of our miscommunications and mistakes. I assumed Jeff understood the anatomy of a garlic clove and Jeff, who had been unsure at the time, thought he'd wing it. This, while small, was certainly a picture of who we were and would continue to be for some time.

Later that same year, we bought our first house and sold the condo in Boston.

20| september 2011

Wyatt had been officially diagnosed with autism just after the age of two, but I knew before then.

At eighteen months, Wyatt was still not talking. Dr. Winwood, his pediatrician, recommended Early Intervention to support him and us at home. Early Intervention provided in-home speech therapy, OT, and social playgroups at their center. This seemed harmless enough. Boys talked late, I had heard, so at first, I was not alarmed.

Early Intervention also hosted weekly parents' groups in the back room of the facility while the kids had their social playgroup. The moms--mostly moms, sometimes dads--would sit around a series of rectangular tables with Lauralie at one end. Lauralie had an oversized personality and heart. She was full of joy, love, and caring. She would hold space to guide parents and caregivers of these special little kids through a discussion on the daily lives with our children; what was hard, what was good, and where did we need help. Most of these children were speech delayed like Wyatt, some had autism, and others had sensory and other specific developmental issues. I had entered a whole new world with a whole new vocabulary, mostly spoken in acronyms. Membership was non-discriminate--all ethnicities, socio-economic standing, and genders were up for grabs.

I attended when I could. The parent group was not a priority for me. I showed up and I listened, but I rarely participated initially. I wanted to believe Wyatt was different than these kids; we would have a different outcome. He would mature. This was not going to be our life--a life of support groups and exceptions. Wyatt would start talking soon, play the sports his dad played, and I'd probably never see these people again. There was no need to get all close and cozy.

I sometimes attended the parent group with Kathryn, Wyatt's nanny at the time. I would head straight into work after group, so I looked the part of the working mom. I showed up acting as if I had my shit together. *I'm only a visitor in this world*, I thought. *We don't belong here.* Underneath, I was drowning in worry and *what ifs*. What if we were not visitors here but actually moving into this with a lifetime membership?

I began to notice Wyatt's consistent shaking of his head. It looked as if he was telling us "no," but no one had asked him a question. I had heard and then googled repetitive movements in children along with lack of eye contact. Something in my gut told me this was my stop in life and that I should unpack and settle in. Intellectually, I started preparing for autism, but no matter what I read, I was not emotionally prepared.

***

Wyatt had been invited to a birthday party for one of my co-worker's daughters, who was a year older than Wyatt. The birthday party was full of little kids all somewhere around Wyatt's age, two-to-five years old. Wyatt was thrilled to see the entire backyard was packed with toys and play structures. He ran from toy to structure, climbing and jumping. He touched and turned over every toy he could get his hands on. This could have been Disneyland as far as Wyatt was concerned. I trailed him wide-eyed, trying to keep up. *Holy hell, this was exhausting.* I was sweating. I looked around to see how other parents were handling this, except, I realized they weren't. No other child was quite like mine. The other parents were observing my son. I was embarrassed. I was an inexperienced mom. They had all been doing a better job managing their children who knew how to control themselves.

I stood motionless watching Wyatt climb up the stairs to the fort for the fifth time. "He sure has a lot of energy," said the woman next to me with a smile--the kind that didn't reach her entire face. I heard the judgment in her voice, and I felt small.

"He does," I agreed. I turned away, stepping closer to the fort. There was an opening at the top that he could fall out of it--or more likely jump out of--if I wasn't watching him. Wyatt had no fear. As I stood eyeing Wyatt's footing on his ascent, I could feel everyone's stares. I needed to leave. In my best mommy voice, I coaxed Wyatt down, and minutes later, we were saying our goodbyes. This would be the shortest birthday party we ever attended--a very long thirty minutes.

Today, I know how to manage and support my son's Attention Deficit Hyperactivity Disorder (ADHD) as well as others' curiosity around it, but back then, I knew nothing. I didn't know Wyatt had ADHD. I felt like I was the worst parent and I wanted to hide. I thought we'd never find our tribe. But I was wrong.

***

In the days and months leading up to the big reveal of Wyatt's autism diagnosis, and eventually, ADHD diagnosis, I became aware how disconnected I felt from my son. I didn't know how to do it like other moms. I tried to engage Wyatt but was failing. Early Intervention had suggested various educational toys to try, so I went on a shopping spree at Lakeshore Learning and bought all of them along with the most colorful, compelling picture flashcards and toys I could find. They were tag-lined with words like "intellectual, stimulating, early learner." I taped these all over the house, so everywhere I walked I could point out to Wyatt some bright, textured picture for him to be inspired to repeat after me, "PPP-ig! Pig!"

Wyatt wasn't talking, but he was throwing tantrums, making utterances they sounded like gibberish, and I couldn't understand him. Wyatt wouldn't look at me either. I couldn't hold his attention. I was creating a poorly-behaved child because I was giving in to his outbursts. Recently, he had bitten me hard and I snapped, without thinking, and I slapped his arm.

What kind of mother was I? Was I working too much? Did I go back too soon? Was that the problem?

At parent's group, I listened to other moms talk about their successes with their children while pangs of jealousy and inadequacy stabbed at me. I wasn't having any of these successes with Wyatt. On a few occasions, I took notes but was hesitant to share what I was feeling or experiencing. I thought I was fooling them by coming off as the put-together career mom.

Work, however, *was* going really well. I was proud of it. We were just about to mark the second year of Business Operations, the group I had built. This was big and important to me as it was proof that what we had created was valued and respected on a level beyond my immediate boss' feedback. The validation puffed me up. I could finally transition to a four-day work week, as I had always intended. Right after maternity leave, I had returned to work with the intention of a four-day week, but I never worked only four days.

One Friday, my day off, I scheduled time for errands and my annual physical. I was pulling down my driveway after my appointment, when I saw Jackie, the Early Intervention specialist, coming down the walkway from my front door. She looked up and waved, her wild curly brown hair blowing in the summer breeze. She gave me a wide-eyed smile and a kind of "oh good, you're here" look. I got out of my car and walked over to meet her. She tended to be chatty, so meeting her outside the house would be best. I was distracted and still sifting through the memory of my doctor's expressions as she probed my neck, feeling my lymph nodes. Had her face been neutral or concerned? Did I see a furrow? One of my lymph nodes was causing her concern. "Let's order an early mammogram," she had said.

"I'm sorry to put you on the spot like this," said Jackie. "I know you're just getting home, but I was hoping we might talk for a few minutes if you have time."

"Sure, what's up?" I smiled.

"Well, the team and I have recently met about Wyatt, and we think he is making great progress." Her voice was steady and her face cheery, but her eyes showed concern. I knew rehearsed when I saw it.

"Yeah, he's really been trying." I nodded, playing along with the script. As I said this, I was thinking, S*ure, but he still isn't talking and he's going to be two years old in two months.*

"So, we are a little concerned about some gaps," Jackie continued.

The no-talking, I wanted to say, *and the head shaking and no eye contact*, my smart-ass internal dialogue rattled off.

"And we think now might be a good time to test him for autism." She paused, looked at me dead on, almost daring me to break eye contact. She was searching me for something.

I wanted to blurt out, *Yeah, it's about time.*

"I agree," I said, in a casual, friendly tone. I smiled. "To be honest, I have been wondering when this might come up," I added, sensing her discomfort. I tried to create an opening for her to relax into. I could tell she needed it.

She sighed, an apologetic smile surfaced, and she explained, "We don't typically like to recommend testing too early; it can really upset some parents."

"Sure, makes sense," I said on autopilot, trying to make her feel better and to end this moment as fast as I could.

Yet, the pregnant pause continued. *What?* I wanted to shout, but, I smiled. "So what's next? What next step should I take?"

Jackie composed herself, standing up a little straighter. She fell back into her script. "I'm heading back to the office now, and as soon as I get there, I will pull some resources for you to call to get Wyatt in for a neuro-psych evaluation. That is the first step. The wait for an appointment can be very long, so I would advise you to call a few places right away to get on a waitlist. Wyatt is so young still, so you might be able to get him in relatively quickly. Actually, there is a practice out in Newton that gives priority testing to younger children. Let me look into that and get back to you," Jackie offered.

"Okay, thank you. I'd appreciate that," I said. I was emotionally detached. The conversation could have been about someone we knew, not my son. Or maybe that was what I had hoped. I had known in the pit of my stomach for a while a conversation like this was approaching, but having it was a different matter. I had even tried to initiate the talk during a few in-home visits by repeatedly noting Wyatt's head movements, trying to get their opinion, but to no avail.

I handled that well, I told myself; emotions in check, no tears.

Jackie continued to look at me--for what? I wondered. There was no way I was going to cry with her. I had been preoccupied with my doctor's appointment. I needed a mammogram ASAP and now this. Did my son have autism? And what if I had cancer? I loved my husband, but Jesus Christ, Jeff by himself with a special needs child would not work. None of this was part of my life's plan, not even a shade of it.

Jackie left finally and backed out of my driveway. I took cover in my house.

"Jeff, I just ran into Jackie out in the driveway," I said as I walked in.

"Yeah, she was asking when you would be home," he said. "Everything okay?"

"I guess. I mean, I don't know. She wants us to get Wyatt tested for autism," I said, trying to seem unphased by busying myself in the kitchen. This should have struck us as odd that Jackie's preference was to talk to me first, but over the past year of working with Early Intervention and having them in our home, the common theme was that they all seemed more comfortable with mom vs. dad. And, in this way it may have further cemented my role of being the lead on all things Wyatt and the world of special needs.

"Well, we have been saying that might be the elephant in the room for a bit right? Jeff asked.

"Right, you're right. It'll be good to know," I said. But I could feel my panic growing, swelling. I needed to pack it up and get out of the house. Jeff was always so damn calm.

"I need to go to Target and pick up a couple of things. Do you need anything?" I asked, picking up my bag again. Jeff probably said *no*, but I didn't even say goodbye before leaving the house. I drove in a fog, my thoughts somewhere between autism and breast cancer. I knew I was being dramatic, but *what if?*

Inside Target, I walked toward the baby aisle on autopilot. The bright baby colors were a collage of pink, blue, and yellow. There was always something I needed to get Wyatt. Aimlessly, I wandered the aisle in a blur of color. Before I knew it, I was at the end of the aisle, where it emptied into the main aisle, and I bumped right into my in-laws. My mother- and father-in-law were with some of my nieces and nephews they often had during the week. Our run-in caught me off guard.

"What are you doing here?" my mother-in-law asked with happy surprise.

"Oh, I'm just buying Wyatt some things for the bathtub.

Nothing special," I lied. I was empty handed.

"And how is Mr. Wyatt?" she asked.

I paused.

"He's good."

I had paused too long. My mother-in-law could see it in my face. Whenever she looked at me with care and concern, it broke me down. There, in the middle of Target's main aisle, in front of everyone, I broke down and started crying big, ugly tears.

My mother-in-law had no idea why I was crying, so she started asking quick, quiet questions. Is everyone safe? Wyatt? Jeff? I needed a minute to catch my breath so I could tell her everyone was fine. Only I wasn't fine; I was scared to death. I was afraid this was my fault--had I done something wrong during my pregnancy? I had been wondering this for a while and had googled it plenty.

I told her everything about Wyatt. "They think he has autism," I said. "I know he does."

Sylvie, as always, remained optimistic. "Well, it doesn't matter. We love him all the same. He is an amazing little boy," she said.

It was true--no matter what the test revealed; he'd still be the boy we loved immensely. He'd be the same child we walked into the appointment with; a paper and a few hours of analysis would not change who he was or the love that surrounded him.

***

The neuropsychological evaluation day came fast. Jackie had been right; we were able to get an earlier appointment because of Wyatt's young age. In the span of a few weeks, breast cancer had been ruled out and autism was now on deck.

"We need to make sure he eats enough breakfast," I said to Jeff the morning of the assessment, as if he was taking a school entrance exam. As if this was a test Wyatt could pass if his belly were full. I was in my head thinking, *get everything right, make sure he eats, make sure he's in a good mood, make sure he'll cooperate, pack a diaper bag, pack snacks, be ready.* Jeff was calm and accommodating to my nerves, his hand on mine.

The drive to the neuropsychologist's office was over an hour. When we arrived, I don't know what I expected, but my first thought was that the doctor's office waiting area could have been cheerier. More welcoming. They had tried to make it seem cozy, but it was more or less a typical waiting room with chairs and a smattering of toys that looked like they were donated from parents or staff. I watched Wyatt and the other kids play; none of them were bothered by the waiting room, but I was irritated. Probably because I already knew in the space that exists at the top of my stomach and below my heart that Wyatt had autism—it's the small hollow spot that echoes the truth throughout the body; it cannot lie.

Dr. Carson and his team came out to greet us. "Mr. and Mrs. Blaeser," a tall, dark-haired man said, walking toward us with his hand extended. His handshake was warm, the two-handed kind. Was this a practiced pre-comforting technique? I wondered.

"Robert," he said with a smile. I appreciated his casual nature and lack of pretense. The team escorted us back to his office where all the testing would take place. The testing procedures were explained, and they reminded me of the tests I could recall from my earliest days of school. Blocks, shapes, sorting, and language drills. Would these really determine such a serious thing as autism?

Jeff and I returned to the waiting room to wait for the next couple of hours. It seemed strange that my little boy, who was still a baby to me, would be left with these strangers for that long for a "test." How would he not be scared? Would he feel like I had abandoned him? I hoped this would be one of those events he would eventually forget that never transformed into a memory. Jeff and I checked our phones, looking over emails for the majority of the time we waited. Every now and again, Jeff would squeeze my hand. Shortly before we were called back into Dr. Carson's office, Jackie, the Early Intervention lead on Wyatt's team, showed up. We had invited her to the appointment to act as a second set of ears, knowing in advance that some of the information we'd be hearing might be overwhelming and very technical.

Two and half hours finally came to an end. We were invited back in Dr. Carson's office sitting on a sofa that was likely sent there after a home re-decorating project in the late nineties. The coffee table between the evaluation team and us was barren, except for a box of Kleenex. I looked at it, feeling a bit of contempt. I wasn't going to need that; I had prepared for the various versions of this meeting. I was controlled and ready.

Dr. Carson and his team were seated in chairs that sat slightly higher than us, giving the meeting a mixed feeling of "feel at home" in his second-hand sofa with a clinical undertone that couldn't be ignored as the team formed a semi-circle opposite us. I sat up taller on the soft sofa. Jeff reached for my hand once again; he knew my tells. As we answered questions about family medical history, I wondered if they were evaluating us, placing bets on which parent was the gene carrier. I was adopted, so *gotcha*, whoever was betting on me loses because we'll never know. I watched them take notes.

They began with what we would soon find was the typical beginning for all such conversations: "Wyatt is an adorable little boy." Then they cut to it--Wyatt was on the spectrum.

I must have been holding my breath because when I finally exhaled it felt like settling into the truth. Words like *might, possibly*, and *potentially* hung in the air, forming a shifting outline of a future of uncertainty. The team continued to share their findings, various statistics, bell curves, and lots of technical terms I would later Google. I took notes and looked at Jackie. I was sure she was catching all the details. She could decode or at least repeat what they were saying so I could re-immerse myself later. My body was in the room, while my head and heart were fighting for control. My uncontrolled fears telescoped in and out of the future. The uncertainty was dizzying and all of my plans I had dreamed were shifting into something different, something fuzzy and unclear. My heart raced but my head would win; it would come up with a new plan.

"Do you have any questions that we can answer right now?" Dr. Carson asked.

Maybe, I thought, but I didn't know what I didn't know. I was holding my breath again and clenching my stomach, physically keeping my shit together. With control and in my best professional voice I asked, "What are the next steps?"

I needed to get a plan in place to help my little boy, to help myself. I didn't look at Jeff because he would know I was wobbling. What if he needed me to be the strong one right now? I could be the strong one so long as I didn't look at him. Looking at him would have revealed that I was on the brink of an emotional landslide. I would not be able to hold up my disguise and carry out my mission to be strong, to be a great mom, to think and plan. There was no time for my messiness right now. There would be time for that later.

Dr. Carson referred us to a developmental pediatrician and armed us with what seemed like the requisite informational packet on autism that had resources for home ABA therapy. The pictures on the pamphlets were of smiling families engaged in happy active lives. What would our life look like, I wondered?

When the appointment was finally over, we stepped outside the doctor's office and the crisp air hit me like an awakening. It was fall. I finally looked at Jeff; he was beside me but not with me. His expression was mostly blank but for an undertone of determination. I knew the look; he was somewhere in his thoughts.

"So, what do you think?" I asked Jeff.

"It's fine. He's still our boy—we'll deal with it," he said and smiled at me.

Jackie looked at me and paused. "Are you okay?" she asked.

"Yes, you know we expected that. Right now, I just want to get the right plan in motion," I said.

"You just seem . . . to be doing . . . really well. I want to make sure that you're actually all right," said Jackie with concern.

"I'm really fine," I assured her with the warmest smile I could paint on. I think I even touched her forearm for effect.

"You're a great mom, you know," said Jackie with a sympathetic smile.

We parted ways. Jeff kissed my forehead and carried Wyatt to the back seat of the car and buckled him into his car seat. I got in the passenger side, thinking to myself, *this will be fine.* As we pulled out of the parking lot, Wyatt began his self-talking babble, and Jeff reached for my hand. There wasn't much of a conversation on our way home except we agreed we weren't surprised by the diagnosis and we were just finally glad to understand what was going on. Neither of us dove in deeper. I would figure out what we needed to do next.

***

Two weeks later, I was in India for work. It was the end of October; I'd be missing the last of the fall colors and Halloween. One night, late, at 10:30 p.m. IST, my hotel room went dark. In fifteen minutes the generator would kick in and the fortunate guests of our five-star hotel would bask in electricity while the majority of Gurgaon would stay dark. I had grown used to this occurrence over the years of traveling to India, but I had never grown comfortable with how visceral the experience was of life's inequities.

I was on a call with my colleague, Clara, and quickly the conversation turned to personal matters. Her father was battling colon cancer and supporting her family weighed heavily on her.

"Family first. Be there for your mom," I said. I thought of Wyatt and Jeff and inventoried all the ways Wyatt's diagnosis might be my fault. The anti-nausea medication during my pregnancy. The paint fumes in the parking garage at work. The pain medication I took when I broke my foot while pregnant.

I pressed mute on the phone as my tears welled up. Why was I here in India and not home with my son, my family? Not that being home would change the autism diagnosis, but Jeff and I had not really talked about how we felt about any of this.

21| june 2016

Lynn, our marriage counselor, was nice, compassionate, and I believe she tried, but in the end, Jeff and I both felt we were overwhelming her with a special needs child, cancer, and a growing distance in our marriage. As we unpacked each of our bits of baggage, Lynn often wore an expression of "wow."

As part of the intake process for counseling with Lynn, each person had a one-on-one session with her. I don't know how Jeff's went, but mine was difficult. Lynn listened with compassion to the broad strokes of my life. I was adopted at an estimated age of eighteen months from Korea. I was an abandoned baby, so my age is a guess. By the age of seven, I had been sexually abused three different times by three different people. It was not until years after the fact that my parents would know about two of the three teenagers, leaving me feeling emotionally unsupported in ways I wasn't even aware at the time I needed. Likely, I admitted, this had an impact on why I tended to detach from my vulnerability. I knew I was loved, but for a host of reasons, I felt marginalized by my family while growing up. On some days, I felt shitty if I looked too closely at some of these memories, but on the other days, I could not deny they were also the birthplace of much of my strength and determination.

Lynn teared up. *Oh, for fuck's sake,* my inner voice sighed. She pitied me, which instantly annoyed me. I didn't recognize it as compassion and shared vulnerability. Lynn's reaction shut me down and falsely reinforced the idea that the stories of my life still had to be censored. When I believed I was on the receiving end of pity, I was my worst self. I walled off, armored up, became tough, and/or pissed.

Lynn's office had two black chairs positioned side by side, where Jeff and I sat for our sessions together. For most of our sessions, I stared at the metal structure on the wall behind Lynn. On this one particular day, however, I was exhausted, and nothing would anchor me--not the deep chair or the metal structure.

"So, how are you?" Lynn inquired.

"Okay," Jeff said. He always said that and if I didn't roll my eyes outwardly, I did mentally.

"Exhausted," I said.

"What's going on?" Lynn asked, directing her question to me.

I sighed. Where should I begin? The house, work catch-up from being out all the time, Wyatt's IEP, Wyatt's perpetual appointments with some specialist or the other, trying to keep up and feel useful to Jeff. Oh, and I generally felt fat.

Everyone handles shit in their life--why was it so hard for me? I really hated Sheryl Sandberg's stupid "Lean In" message. I leaned in and, in the process, pulled away from everything else. I hoped Lynn wasn't a Sheryl fan.

"Everything. I don't even know where to begin. I just have so much to do all the time," I said.

"Well, what would it be like if you didn't do any of it?" Lynn asked happily. Was she high? Clearly, she was not a Sheryl fan.

"It would be a complete shit show because then nothing would get done," I replied. I wasn't about to sugar coat this.

I didn't even have to sideways glance at Jeff to know I had made him feel bad for Lynn. She had bumped into Team B. Jeff was Team A, the nice one in our relationship. I was Team B, the crazy, precise one who got shit done and, in the process, made people feel uncomfortable. We had taken to joking about us in this way, but it wasn't really a joke. The truth of it pissed me off. Being Team B was sucking the life out of me. Why couldn't I be Team A? I had tried a version of "don't do any of it" a couple of years ago when I had left the consultancy. But not working, not doing any of it felt wrong too.

It was May 2014 when I left my career at the consultancy, choosing to be home with Wyatt. For the better part of four months I had wrestled with the decision of career versus full-time motherhood on my yoga mat. This was one of the most difficult decisions of my adult life. Somewhere between arm balances and savasana, I saw and felt ways in which I was better at my job than being a mom. My instincts at my job were stronger and more confident. And my old priority to kick ass at work had changed. The priority now was to be a good mom. I *needed* to be a better mom.

In 2009 when Wyatt was born, I had taken the allotted six weeks of maternity leave, but as soon as it was over, I had been eager to get back to work. In fact, I could not wait to take on a new challenge and more responsibility that was being offered to me. Back then, I was ready to kick ass. I knew how to do my job. I was getting good at it. Motherhood, on the other hand, scared the shit out of me. Outsourcing part of it to a qualified nanny seemed like a smart idea. I rationalized Wyatt was so young he'd never remember who was there or not. But magically, day by day, my son had imprinted so deeply on my heart that I saw every part of him and his needs, and despite my insecurities about being a mom, I was pulled toward him. Wyatt was special and he needed more of me. The universe had given him to me as my real job, and I had been underperforming. I hoped that removing the stress of my job would be an added bonus and that I would become a nicer person and could focus more on my marriage. I would practice yoga, be light, joyful, and less stressed. Afterall, over the years, my yoga practice had connected me to or at least shown me parts of who I was and helped me see what I needed. I would be more Team A.

Embracing my truth, we let Kathryn the nanny go (which was maybe as hard if not harder than leaving my career—she handled the parts that I was afraid of failing at, like potty training, effortlessly), and I left my career. I became more focused all right, but on the fact that Jeff and I had stopped talking about anything besides Wyatt. We stopped laughing, connecting, and understanding one another. Then my great idea to build a house together turned out to be a pretty bad one. In hindsight, I think Jeff got on board because he thought it would keep me from being bored since I had left work. All these assumptions and to-do lists were burying us. It was like standing too close to a Georges Seurat painting--all you see are the dots, but not the full picture.

Back then, I was the stay-at-home mom who rarely stayed at home, between Wyatt's appointments and family errands. Things to do sprouted like a bunch of mushrooms after a rainstorm. What I hated more, though, was the difference in the way people engaged with me when they first met me. The old version of me--the working-mom version--was interesting and I was admired for juggling and "doing it all." With the new version, people weren't curious who I was beyond being a mom. When I explained I was a full-time mom, the flicker of interest in their eye waned and their interest in me dimmed. This annoyed the piss out of me, and I fought the urge to justify my very being with stories of world travel and an account of how many of the Seven Wonders I had seen--six to be exact. I wanted to tell them I read non-fiction with the same veracity as fiction. And, my ego wanted them to know, a couple of years ago they would have LinkedIn me in short order. I had been damn good at my job.

Lynn wasn't going to be put off by my attitude, she jumped back in smiling and served the ball right back to me,

"Well, are there any parts, any things, that maybe you could not do or ask for help with?" she asked kindly. I looked at Jeff. I knew what she was getting at. No, the idea of catching him up on how to do everything *right*, i.e. my way, was more exhausting than doing it myself.

"No," I said, feeling the sad latch of a door shutting to keep me trapped in a room with my anger and perfection.

Jeff looked at me with tired but willing eyes. "Let me help. I'll do whatever you tell me to do," he said. But I knew I wouldn't. Even as I lied and said I would think about it, the risk was too great. I needed the pieces of our life to be neat and tidy more now than ever. I was not willing to let anyone but me have control.

Going back to work engaged my brain and quieted my ego, but I still tried to play the role of perfect mom, running around like a chicken with my head cut off. I rushed home from work in Boston to Wyatt's social skills play groups. I was also trying to be the best, supportive wife to my sick husband, attending doctor and chemo appointments, and all the while, I was emotionally falling apart at the seams. I didn't and couldn't talk to anyone about how I was focused simply on survival and moving through my days checking boxes. I was afraid talking about it might break my resolve. My busyness kept me afloat, but it was also making me resentful. I was tired and asking for help seemed like more work. I sounded like my mom, who would occasionally get disgusted with our family of six and would say, "I'll just do it myself!"

Marriage counseling ended and it's hard to say if the timing was wrong or if it was just wrong for us. My reserved husband was not the type to discuss the discomfort of our marriage or his discomfort with me with a third party. And I was mad and pissed off, but mostly sad, wrapped in a layer of dread. Our days melded, one into the next, as we operated in survival mode. A self-imposed deadline lingered--the pressure to make us perfect and happy by the time chemo was over, but, I wondered, what if Jeff was still sick in six months? We had to be in a better place by then for his emotional health and mine.

22| july 2016

On Wednesday just before the fourth of July weekend in 2016 we finally started the process of moving. Wednesday was Jeff's scheduled chemo day, so I had to miss his session. July also meant Jeff was entering his third month of chemo, halfway through his prescribed six months of treatment. By now, Jeff was visibly tired most of the time and his hair had thinned. He had cut his hair to a short crew cut so the hair loss would be less obvious. We had worried that Wyatt might notice Jeff's aggressively thinning hair and ask questions, but we had agreed not to talk about Jeff's cancer with Wyatt unless our hand was forced.

I hadn't missed a chemo session yet, and when I envisioned Jeff by himself in his souped-up recliner, it hurt my heart. So, I did the next best thing I could think of and I asked his dad to accompany him. Knowing my father-in-law would be there in my place gave me peace of mind. This, of course, was not something I had run by Jeff; he would have never agreed to anyone doing anything for him.

Caroline, the new nanny, came over at 7:00 a.m. She was the quintessential millennial, always going with the flow of things. The toys and moving boxes in my chaotic apartment were simply things for her to step around. She was unflappable, which was perfect for my six-year-old hurricane. Caroline got Wyatt ready for school, managing his daily protests of not wanting to go and requests for "two more minutes." Mornings in our apartment resembled a flash flood--abrupt madness and commotion transitioning to dead silence the second the door shut and Wyatt was on the other side of it. That day was no different.

Once the two of them left, I stood alone in the apartment scanning the remaining items to be packed. My heart sank with disappointment. Lego structures, books, pots, and pans were still everywhere. Despite the boxes littered about, my packing efforts in the previous weeks looked half-assed, as my dad might have assessed. The apartment was tiny and packed to the gills; there was no more room to stack packed boxes, so I had given up a few days back. We had lived through several gift-giving holidays (and much receiving in Wyatt's case) in the apartment, which meant the toy inventory had grown quite a bit since we had moved in over a year ago, and then, as if right on cue, my mother-in-law arrived.

Sylvie was not empty handed; she came armed with moving boxes (the right kind with handles), tape, scissors, and packing paper. She had been to the rodeo and yielded her life experience with the functionality and proficiency of a Swiss Army knife. Most people show up with the intention to help, but they create work because you need to direct and explain, but not Sylvie. She got shit done, and more times than not, had better ideas on how to do it than you did. I admired this about her.

I often marveled at how she had six kids, thirteen grandchildren, and was able to move quickly and readjust without missing a mark. I saw similarities between her and my mom at times, too. Maybe if you do a job long enough, you just become good at it. After all, they had been wives and mothers much longer than me.

Sylvie carefully assessed Wyatt's large Lego structures and how we might move them without damage. We stared at the Lego City Police Station and Sylvie determined this one would need to be partially disassembled and put back together later. I had concerns, but Sylvie was certain Aaron my nephew would be able to remedy any missteps.

The two of us packed, rolling various items in paper and bubble-wrap, then tested the weight of boxes before taping them closed. In no time, the apartment was once again the sterile, sufficient space we had moved into. I was surprised by how much of a home we actually had made this apartment into during the time we occupied it. The dining room wall looked sad without Wyatt's colorful Word Wall cluttering it. The flash cards of sight words and word families were all down. As was the rewards chart to mark Wyatt's progress. On most days this "clutter" drove me nuts and was just another thing that made the space feel like it was closing in on me, but today, in the absence of its normal clutter, I saw it for what it was--the sweet details of my life. My phone binged with a text from the builder. He was finally ready to do the walkthrough of the house. Sylvie and I stopped what we were doing to drive over to the new house.

Ten minutes later, we pulled into the driveway. The house should have struck me as pretty with its sage green color and white trim, the deep blue front door, and farmer's porch. I wanted to love it, but the porch's elevation was too high and the landscaping package was lacking because I hadn't had time to work with the landscaper on something better. The builder, in a golf shirt and jeans, was waiting for us next to his white pickup truck. He looked like he was ready to head off for the long fourth of July weekend. He rarely looked the part of a builder. I think he had stepped out of the executional role some time ago and was more focused on the financial end of the project. We wasted little time after I introduced my mother-in-law and headed into the house.

We entered through the back door off of the garage, which led into the mudroom. The house smelled like new wood, paint, and stain. The majority of the walls were painted various shades of gray, according to the color key I had provided. The protective plastic film had been removed from the windows and bright sunlight flooded the house. I was relieved to see the floors were stained beautifully. In the days before I had noticed they looked dull from all the workman foot traffic. The house looked lovely, however, I couldn't shake the disappointment gnawing at the back of my mind. Despite my best efforts, I saw the discrepancies and imperfections. I was wired to see them. More than a year of bickering with the builder had done me in and no material thing was worth the fighting and drama that had ensued. I was disappointed in myself for how I had let this project piss me off so much. Deep down, I knew this was not about the house, but my need to win. Jeff had told me over and over again, "It does not matter what the contract says. There are some things the builder just has the upper hand on, so let it go. He's going to do the right thing or he's not--you can't control it."

The builder stood across from me at the kitchen island. I knew I had to be nice and complimentary, so I channeled Sylvie's grace and way of managing life with strength and a smile.

I had heard stories about how builders could leave you in the lurch over punch lists and surprise owners with overages. I was sure this was not over.

The builder called me out on "trust" as I pulled out my binder of paperwork. He had nothing with him, saying he didn't like to work "that way." There was no love between us and any trust that had existed had been eroded to the point of no return, so I was confused by what he thought was him taking the high road. I had tried several times to consider what it might be like to be him. He had a sizable development in progress in the adjacent town and likely, trying to please everyone when all you do is custom builds had to be a tiring business. I knew people could be jerks; I wasn't immune from this, but still, over the past year and half he had likely out done me in that department.

I looked past him into the family room at the rocked fireplace where, on either side of it, two large empty cavities glared at me like double middle fingers. This was supposed to be built-in shelving, scoped and contracted, but the builder contended that no one told him what to build. He gave us a $3,000 credit and months later, we paid his guy on the side $9,000 to build them.

By this point I was run down and he knew it. There were other disappointments and missing items; radiant heating in a bathroom, crown molding, a firepit, and incorrect appliances. Adding to what felt like an endless flow of insults, overages were drawn up, which had no change orders. We had been warned by our attorney this would likely happen--they would be small enough to swallow, but large enough to be annoying. And they were. But Jeff and I didn't have the energy for any more fighting. We had bigger priorities in our lives.

I thought about the change of address card we might send out. It wouldn't be beautiful like the ones other people send, with the whole family on the front porch, all smiling, holding a sign that says, "We've moved!" Mine would be a selfie giving our new house the middle finger.

I decided, in the end, to send nothing.

***

The move took two days. The finish on the floors needed to set one more day before we could walk on them or put anything heavy on them, so all the furniture would be moved into the garage. The closing and lease-end of our apartment was just before the fourth of July weekend, so we had to book two moving companies, as neither company was available both days.

Everything from the apartment fit into the two-car garage, stacked up and probably sustaining some level of damage from the weight of it all. On the second day, we returned, and moving company number two brought the bulk of our possessions out of long-term storage. Our life began to move and spread into the house. My stickering and labeling of the boxes made fast work of their delegation to the appropriate rooms, thanks to Pinterest life hacks. The rooms in the house were also labeled accordingly so the movers could place everything in its designated room. I am sure they thought I was neurotic, but I was dealing with special circumstances, and everyone needed to follow directions.

Jeff was only one day off of his chemo, but he tried to help. He made me nervous. I wanted him to sit. This was generally the day his treatment would catch up to him. Jeff would slow down; his eyes would fall heavy--a sign that he felt worse. Jeff never shared this with me, but his body made it clear. I could manage the movers myself and his mom had returned, so we had this.

Sylvie directed movers like a pro and had the foresight to bring bottled waters and order pizzas for them. I continued to stress over Jeff, fearing what he was doing to his body, but he would not sit still. In hindsight, I wondered if we should have stayed in the apartment a month longer so it would have been just the tiniest bit less chaotic. But the burning need to start something new in our lives was strong and thirty more days seemed like a life sentence.

Once the movers had done their part, it took an additional three days to settle into the house before we moved into it as a family. Jeff and I worked tirelessly while Sylvie watched over Wyatt and I watched over Jeff. "Sit. Please, rest. I can do this," I said to Jeff over and over, as I unpacked dishes and made my rounds throughout the house, sorting through our belongings. Jeff was restless, so eventually I gave in, and he was assigned video game console setup, along with a few other small, lightweight tasks.

Wyatt's room had to be perfect and sorted before we moved in. Change was hard for Wyatt and if he did not have immediate access to the things that gave him comfort, shit would hit the fan. Toys, stuffed animals, and oversized bean bag chairs were set up in a perfect, cozy arrangement. I hoped he would take to his new home. Wyatt liked consistency and even more than that, Wyatt liked and needed his space. A place to decompress and reset soothed him.

I was way past exhaustion and if I had had the energy to cry, I might have. I was the rock that skims across the pond--it can't slow down because once it does, it sinks.

During the transition, we stayed at Joe and Sylvie's house. This was not what I had planned. I had envisioned the move would be slow and gradual, like on an HGTV show. In my vision, I would have had time to set up over the course of a week like a house stager, but it would be my house. We'd live in the apartment until I was done. I'd have it all planned with dates marked on a calendar. I loved a good plan; it was my catnip, however, it was a relief to be at Joe and Sylvie's familiar home. The mornings were peaceful and quiet and having coffee and breakfast with the two of them became my unexpected snuggly blanket.

The morning of the fourth of July, I stood looking out the expanse of windows in their living room that offered a sweeping view of the backyard. It was breathtaking. The sun rose over the lake, the horseshoe-shaped garden where Jeff and I had said our vows--in sickness and health, forever--was front and center in full bloom. *Yes, forever*, I thought. We are forever. Moments like these always struck me, as I would have never guessed then the future would be even a close shade of what it was today. All the effort, the worry, the planning--for what? We had landed at a different destination. This new, different place wasn't necessarily worse— well, cancer was worse for sure--but some parts were amazing. I never imagined that having a child with special needs would open my heart so wide and make my life so hard while at the same time so much better. Wyatt had been a gift, his life a classroom for my soul. His differences were not entirely the same as mine were, but in some ways, I saw the similarities. I was different as a child, too. I knew what it felt like to feel different. I didn't know then what precisely that feeling was, but I knew now. When I held Wyatt in my thoughts, it was clear to me that my mission was to give him enough love and acceptance at home so the outside world would seem like a distraction rather than a thing to chase or see as a place of failed expectations.

***

Slowly the weeks passed, and our new home took on a lived-in feeling. Wyatt's toys sprawled in a mess across the floors and new furniture was delivered. The deep, comfy gray sofa arrived about the same time as the navy blue bar stools. We now had places to sit other than on the one recliner gifted by Sylvie to Jeff and aptly anointed The Chemo Recovery Chair and the two oversized bean bag chairs, temporarily commandeered from Wyatt's playroom. Familiar decorative pieces from travel and our life before were placed in new spots: the jade family ball from China for good luck, various items from India, framed maps, and my old white office furniture in the first-floor office overlooking where the firepit was now being built, by a local contractor. Our lives settled over the house like a new shade of color called "us."

Our neighbors were unexpectedly sweet. In the first few weeks, the doorbell rang intermittently, and a friendly face would welcome us to the neighborhood with flowers or baked goods. I had never been very social outside of a professional setting, not in years anyway. Friendly for the sake of friendly I liked, but I sucked at it and therefore felt like a fish out of water. Most of my life I had played at fitting in, but I had come to accept my failure at true social belonging. What could I possibly talk about that would be interesting for an extended period of time? After talking on calls all day at work, I was sick of hearing my own voice.

I got the sense this neighborhood genuinely liked each other and were real friends. It made me feel unsteady. When I was in my twenties, I had mastered the illusion of excellent social skills. I could throw a party or fill a bar with people I knew for Thursday night drinks, my trick being that I was a "curator of people." I connected and introduced people and only stayed in conversations long enough to solicit interests and then connect them to another like-minded person. I was pretty sure, however, this party trick wouldn't work anymore.

***

I took a leave of absence from work for the month of July. I needed the mental and emotional reset; the wheels weren't falling off yet, but they were wobbling and feeling out of alignment.

Jeff developed a work schedule around his chemo appointments with some down days for recovery. This grated on me because I thought he should take more time off to take care of himself. If not now, when? When Jeff was home, I saw the exhaustion in his eyes, his half-awake expression, the tentative way he moved and the huff or exhale he'd unconsciously release as he eased into a chair. This is how we lived now. I watched for any change in his health. I tried to feel compassion for what I considered must be a loss of control having to follow doctor's orders and hoping his own silent prayers would be answered. I knew he wanted to be strong. I didn't want to take away any reserves he was holding onto, so I kept my worries to myself.

Most days, Jeff and I politely lived around each other. Outward anger didn't seem to be a dial setting for Jeff and me; it was an agreement I had made with myself about the kind of marriage I wanted long ago. I never wanted us to be the kind of people who yelled at each other or said mean things. That stuff-- even if forgiven--is rarely forgotten.

We remained two people focused on trying to keep life as normal as we could for our son and comfortable for each other.

Our conversations were cordial and measured and completely unmemorable. Jeff treated me with appreciation. But appreciation for what? He rarely let me do anything for him. Not unless I could anticipate it and get it done before him. This way of being around each other created a version of me that never turned off. My mind turned endlessly trying to anticipate what he needed, and in doing so, I watched him like a hawk. I hung on his every word, searching for clues as to how he was feeling. We never talked outright about how he felt or the "C" word. Our short stint in couples counseling consisted of me doing the talking. Even skilled, professional Lynn could not crack Jeff open. And I was shut out.

I could tell by Jeff's quick, discrete actions in caring for the colostomy bag that he was uncomfortable with it still, but also, he never complained. This was another thing we did not talk about. I steered clear of his daily routine as much as I could. I worried about him feeling emasculated. In the hospital, early on, I learned how to care for and change the colostomy bag if I ever needed to, but I knew my husband and he would likely die before he'd ask me to help him. Jeff was a private person. On occasion, my decision to pee with the master bathroom door open, even after ten years of marriage, still made him mildly uncomfortable.

As the chemo treatments took their toll on Jeff physically, they took a toll on my nerves. Neuropathy, sometimes experienced as numbness and weakness, is a side effect chemo and it started to set into Jeff's hands as well as his legs. I became aware Jeff was experiencing this problem when I was in the kitchen getting Wyatt's typical gourmet dinner of chicken nuggets and French fries ready when I heard a loud thundering down the stairs. *Holy Christ*, I thought, as I ran to the front hall.

"Jeff?" I yelled.

"I'm fine," he said.

As I rounded the corner, my six-foot-three husband was sitting on one of the bottom steps. I looked at him, shocked, but knowing.

Jeff looked deflated. "I tripped," he said.

"You tripped or you fell?" I asked. I could hear myself--I sounded pissed. I knew I needed to check my tone, but I was scared it could have been so much worse, and when I was scared, I sounded mad.

"I stumbled a little. My legs are just a little weak lately," he admitted. My heart raced. *Shit.* We just built this damn house with our bedroom upstairs, another bad choice I berated myself for.

"Daddy?" Wyatt came around the corner from upstairs.

"We're fine monkey," I said.

"I'm fine bug," Jeff said with a smile.

Wyatt had oddly taken to the two nicknames we used for him interchangeably since he was a baby.

"What happened? Did you fall?" he asked.

"Just slipped. I'm fine," said Jeff.

"Okay, be careful," Wyatt added and went back into his room.

I wanted to be that accepting, but I wondered what else Jeff wasn't telling me.

Jeff didn't tell me in the week leading up to his ER visit that his stomach was off and he didn't feel right. That stomachache that turned out to be cancer. I had found him in the middle of the night, on the couch, drenched in sweat with a fever.

"Why are you out here?" I had whispered. Seeing him on the sofa, my first thought was, *are things that bad?* We weren't as close as we had been, but I didn't think we were at the point of sleeping separately.

"I didn't want to wake you. I have a stomachache. I'm fine," he said.

I reached down and touched his forehead. It was sweaty. He was burning up.

"You're not fine. You need to go to the doctor. You have a fever. At a minimum, you have an infection."

"Okay, I'll go after work tomorrow." If I couldn't trust Jeff to know his body, how would I know I could trust him when he said thing were going to be fine?

***

My parents came from Tennessee to visit in July while I was on leave from work. They wanted to be helpful.

"We're doing great," I said, and hugged my mom in the baggage claim of Logan International Airport. Both my parents looked excited and happy to be here.

"And Jeff, how's Jeff?" my Dad asked.

"Good. He's good. Tired, but handling everything well enough," I said. I could have unloaded my dramatic, tearful story on them if I knew how to. Jeff was not telling me how he was actually feeling and I was nervous all the time. But in my mind, I believed they were more comfortable with a stronger version of me. It was the version I had built and practiced the most with them in recent years. I finally had grown up and put away parts of our past- -the girl who cried about everything behind her locked bedroom door while scribbling endless pages in her journal. And when I became a smart-mouthed teenager, I decided to stop needing them. As an adult, I believed I had convinced them I was tough, so how could I admit now I might actually need them? What if revealing myself as weak and dependent disappointed them? What if I was still the ridiculous, imperfect girl my brothers had called "guppy lips"? I heard *I told you so* in the back of my mind. The more I questioned myself, the more I reasoned that they didn't really want the truth, and I described a more palatable version of my life.

"And Wyatt, how is my little grandson?" my mom asked.

"Good. In summer school, says he hates it, but I'm not sure he does. You know kids and school." I tried to sound positive, but I thought maybe it was true, that Wyatt did hate it. I mean, I would have. What kid wanted to go to school year-round and make crappy crafts?

Wyatt loved spending time with his grandparents as he had not seen them in three years. It was fun to watch my mom with him, the very same woman who had zero interest using an iPad or email was playing Super Mario Galaxy and Mario Cart on the Wii with Wyatt. Just when I thought I had my mom pegged, the peg came loose. They laughed and competed fiercely. My mom knew how to love children and they loved her.

23| end of summer – fall 2016

Reluctantly, I returned to work after my short leave of absence. During my commute into Boston, I'd think about the day ahead and it made me anxious. I had been disengaged from my job too long and out too frequently. The month off, leaving early, and the doctors' appointments left me feeling behind. *You can't do this, everyone is carrying you,* whispered my self-doubt as its best friend, guilt, chimed in. My personal shit-storm had kicked up just as I was starting to get my footing and learn this new job seven months ago, but since then my focus had been off.

I found a cure for the noise in my head--it was Audible. I began to listen to audiobooks on my drive to work for a distraction and it worked.

Most days, once I stepped off the elevator, I was able to put on my game face and be a different person at work. But on other days, once I cocooned myself in my office and began reading emails and reviewing project details, my anxious voice would start to stir. *I can't catch up. I can't do this.* I was sure this was showing up in meetings. *Dig in,* I told myself. I knew how to work through the hard stuff. I was good at getting shit done.

My mind battled itself endlessly. Was staying at the investment firm being selfish? And who was I actually helping? But I didn't want to quit another job for my personal life. I had left the software consulting firm and all of its hard won successes to be home for

Wyatt. If I left for home again, I'd be seen as nothing. Jeff would get better soon, we were almost there, and he wouldn't need me anymore. Then, If I didn't work, where was my value? I wondered if the investment firm wanted me to leave. They probably wouldn't fire me. I couldn't imagine John doing that now. But I didn't want to put him in that position either. I needed to do the right thing, but the right thing for who? A little more time, give it a bit more time, see if you can pull it together, I told myself.

***

Outside of work, I was anxious over things I had never considered before. I developed this crazy notion that if Jeff did not get home right on time, he was obviously dead on the side of the road in some car crash. One night, I remember calling Jeff's cell to find out where he was. He should have been home twenty minutes ago. If he answered, I reasoned, everything was fine.

He didn't answer. It went straight to voicemail. My mind took off exploring the most awful conclusions. If he had been in an accident would the police know to look for his phone? Was I listed in his contacts as "wife?" In my mind's eye, he had crashed his car texting or checking email. I sat staring at the clock, paralyzed, as I tried to rationalize my fears. I knew I was being crazy.

When Jeff finally arrived home thirty minutes later, I unleashed my wrath because he didn't answer his phone when I called.

"You could have called to let me know you were running late!" I snapped with zero explanation. Jeff, forgiving and non-confrontational, was unphased.

"Oh, sorry." He paused, looking around the kitchen as if there was some logical reason hidden there that would indicate why I was acting insane. "I got caught up at work," he said.

I was tired and didn't know how to keep up the façade. I

wanted to be strong and run up to the end of the year like a smiling, effortless wife. My Facebook feed was full of stories about these heroic people juggling life's punches and still kicking ass. Why not me? I had moments of perfect engagement, but they were inconsistent. I kept trying harder, but I was falling apart.

***

The leaves on the trees turned orange and red, marking the end of summer and the start of fall. I loved the colors and smells of fall, signaling that change was right around the corner. This year, fall meant Jeff's chemo treatments were coming to an end. Fear--the uninvited guest who had crawled up inside of my heart the day I sat on the bathroom floor at the Northshore General Hospital--was still kicking around. These days, it sat in the pit of my stomach. I tried to hold the finish line in my mind's eye. If we made it, it would be our something wonderful, wouldn't it?

I considered Jeff's remaining chemo and doctor appointments the same way I managed a project plan with dependencies and risks. I needed statuses on everything. Jeff played along as much as he could, giving me executive-level status updates. The big doctor appointment with the oncologist in November was the light at the end of the tunnel where we would see if the chemo had successfully killed any and all micro-cancer cells. Once Jeff received a clean bill of health, he would have one more major surgery, the colostomy reversal. I looked forward to the end of the year as it held hope and, unfortunately, hope's ugly distant cousin, uncertainty. I needed everything to be okay. I was not ready to face it if wasn't, but I was also becoming aware that I would never be ready.

With the regular school year back in session came the monthly IEP check-ins with Wyatt's teacher. In addition, it also kicked off the cycle of Wyatt's regular doctor appointments, every six weeks with the developmental pediatrician, neuropsychologist, and pediatrician, annually. Not to mention his ongoing speech, OT, and social skills groups. Life was a whirlwind of busy, and it was hard to put my finger on any one thing that was making me more annoyed than the other. Even the long-awaited, now-complete house was making me nuts. My friends and family were excited, but I held the house in contempt. It was another thing that had created tension in my life and it still needed my attention: rugs, blinds, wall art. I took my anger out on a plant, deprived it of water, and let it die.

Mid-October brought with it an end to Jeff's six months of chemotherapy treatment. My mind and heart did happy jumps.

"Hey, want to celebrate the end?" I asked Jeff.

"We don't need to do anything. I'm just happy it's over," he said.

And that was the end of it. This was Jeff: low key, no fanfare, no desire for attention.

The "big" doctor's appointment followed shortly after and it consisted of blood work and scans. Jeff, Joanna--Jeff's longtime friend and oncology nurse--and I sat with Dr. Downing, his oncologist. I was anxious but hopeful. I had asked Joanna to sit in on the appointment to help us listen. Much of this was still overwhelming to me, and by now, I knew where I fell short. Dr. Downing met with us in a regular patient exam room, she smiled and looked Jeff square in his eyes. "Everything looks great," she said. "We see no cancer." The six months of chemotherapy had been a success. Dr. Downing cautioned that she would not call Jeff in remission for three years. Jeff would need three years of clean test results, but right now, Jeff had a clean bill of health. Also, we were acutely aware that if any of the micro-cancer cells had spread from the tumor perforation, it was highly likely the spread would show up within the next twelve months. But Dr. Downing was very optimistic.

Everyone exhaled with relief. We all sat a bit taller and smiled. I looked at Jeff. He had a look of satisfaction on his face. In a different universe, I would have run over and hugged my husband, but in this universe, I stayed where I was. *What if it comes back?* We had years of testing ahead of us. The tight tug of anxiety was like a rip cord that accelerated my heart beat just the tiniest bit, and I heard the whispers of worry. I tried to quiet them and stay in the moment and celebrate this day we had been hoping for for the better part of a year.

Our families and friends were overjoyed; it was great news. I kept telling myself, *Be* happy, but I was afraid to believe it.

24| november 2016

Jeff's reversal surgery was scheduled for the first week of December. Jeff would have the colostomy bag removed, and they would reconnect his descending colon back to the rest of his body. The recovery period would last the whole month of December, accompanied by bed rest. I considered our house, the stairs, Jeff's failing legs, and his unwillingness to share with me the real state of this body, specifically if he felt pain. I could not trust him. I would need to be there with him because too many things could go wrong. He could get an infection or fall down the stairs again.

Jeff had been waiting for this green light, the last step in getting his life back. I knew he was self-conscious and always worried about the colostomy bag rupturing. I thought about how I might show my happiness for him. I wanted him to know I knew it was a big deal to have it removed, procedurally and emotionally, and I needed him to feel supported. Ultimately, I played the removal down and focused on the aftercare. I was concerned he might mistake my happiness for him as me having issues with it, with him.

I would need to take time off work again but taking another month off after only working at the firm for eight months didn't sit right with me. Work had been generous and understanding, but at some point, I needed to be responsible for what I knew needed to be done. I would have to quit. I hated quitting, however, it was the right thing to do. The projects needed full coverage and I needed to support my husband in the best way I knew how. Plus, I couldn't say for certain if in six months there wouldn't be another shit storm to contend with. I was always chasing a finish line that kept moving just as I rounded the corner. The feeling of failure by quitting overwhelmed me, but I couldn't deny that it also was an escape hatch relieving some of the pressure I was feeling.

On the day I gave my notice, I drove into work with scattered incoherent thoughts. I was listening to *God's Banker* on Audible--a dense account of the Catholic church's money issues and corruption when the "what ifs" wafted into my head. *What if John thinks I am the biggest flake ever? What if I can never get a job again? What if I regret this?* The first time I worked for John at the software consulting firm, he convinced me to stay and as a result, he helped me find my way and grow up a bit in the process. But this time, I wasn't young and undirected anymore, I was just untethered.

My office was located diagonally across from John's. The exterior walls of the office were frosted glass but clear on the bottom. I had discovered I could peer into John's office and seeing his two black loafers indicated he was in. Out of the corner of my eye, I noticed movement and saw his feet.

"One. Two. Three. Go." I got up, locked my monitor, and headed over to his office. "Have a minute?" I asked as I stood in his doorway, clinging to it like a life raft. John looked up. "I do," he said in his normal, even tone. A part of me hated dumping this on him first thing, but I needed to be done with it. Technically, I reported to one of his direct reports, but I felt like I owed him an explanation first. I could still remember the day we talked on the phone about me coming to work on his team. I had been mindlessly staring out the windshield of my car in the pick-up line at the elementary school when my phone rang. I was thrilled that he would consider me to work for him again.

Like déjà vu of so many years ago, I sat across from John at his desk. My eye contact was terrible. I gazed beyond his head--out his window at the city view and then eventually down at my hands resting on my lap as I explained my cutting tail and needing to leave. Older, more mature now, or maybe just more tired, I didn't try to hide how small and defeated I felt. I slouched in the chair. I was honest about my not being able to do it all. The work and my life were at odds. At this point, I had known John far too long to be anything but honest and likely my resignation was a bit of an emotional purge. I couldn't let go of the guilt for being out so often and the overwhelming feeling of coming up short, and I was done trying to pull it off. I needed to claim responsibility for my reality and be grateful for the accommodations I had been given that an employee of eight months didn't really deserve. Taking responsibility had a way of giving me back a semblance of control and dignity. I can't recall the exact words of the conversation, but I remember John being generous with appreciation for my work. He was thanking me, which of course nearly made me cry.

I gave the firm a month's notice so that I could transition and train a replacement. Nothing was more important to me than the way I left things from that point on. My last day was marked with a team lunch. We were seated in the middle of the restaurant at the Palm. My team took turns going around the table saying complementary things in my honor. In my mind, I had failed and didn't understand how they could say nice things about me. My gaze fell to the white tablecloth and I waited for them to end.

The week before Jeff's reversal surgery, we hosted a holiday party at the house. It was somewhat impromptu, but a nice close to a year that needed to be packed away and forgotten. Hopefully, it was the worse year we would ever have.

Jeff and I continued with our politeness. Our connection to each other had gotten lost in all the drama of our life, and we had made an unspoken agreement to fill its space with hollow, friendly formalities.

We were watching TV one night when Jeff asked, "How would you feel about having some people over, a small holiday thing?"

He surprised me. This was atypical for him. He was quiet and not a party thrower. But if he wanted to celebrate, I was in.

"Yeah, sure, when?" I asked.

"Next week?" he asked.

Right before his surgery. This pulled at my heart and I immediately set about that night reaching out to the friends he wanted me to invite.

The following Friday night arrived and we had a house full of friends drinking wine and eating finger foods. I was glad for the distraction as it was also my last week of work. The diversion kept my pity party from taking over. Most of our friends had not been to the new house. The evening was fun and having friends in our home felt right. I liked seeing Jeff socializing, smiling easily. From across the room, he looked confident, like the man I met years ago. My husband was happy and handsome and it made me smile.

***

The morning of the reversal surgery, Sylvie came to the house to get Wyatt off to school. We were officially nanny-free now once again as I was no longer employed. Jeff and I drove to Northshore General Hospital. The sun had barely begun to rise. I was accustomed to this part of the morning from my former commute. I watched the horizon as the smallest slivers of white and yellow emerged. It was like every other day to the rest of the world. I don't remember much conversation on the drive, likely we talked about Christmas and Wyatt's ever-growing list of wants. We had a way of filling our awkward silences with Wyatt-talk.

We pulled into the parking garage at Northshore General Hospital. We had not been back there together since leaving nine months ago digesting the word *cancer*. This place made me feel breakable. My strength was only on the surface. I had a million little cracks just beneath my smile that could turn into nervous tears at any indication of kindness.

I sat in pre-op with Jeff, but it felt different than the last time. It was more relaxed, no controlled whispers in the background. I told myself not to feel dread; this would be fine. I practiced deep, intentional breathing. The past was bumping around in my chest. Jeff--in his white-and-blue-polka-dotted hospital gown--looked healthy to me. He had gained weight over the past couple of months. He was alert, not drugged on morphine. "I think I might be interested in interior architecture," I said. I had been thinking about this quietly for a little while now. I knew leaving my job would leave a gap in my life and I needed a plan for that space and time. I wasn't good without something to wrap my mind around. A little time back in a classroom might do the trick.

"You'd be great at it. You did a great job with the house," Jeff said, always my cheerleader.

I smiled, uncomfortable with the compliment. I knew I had thrown in the towel on the house once the shit had hit the fan.

"I don't know about that, but I was thinking about taking a course at the Boston Architectural College just to keep my mind engaged," I said. While I was glad for a little time off, it scared me--who was I now?

"I just want to see if I actually think it's interesting," I added, trying not to sound too invested in the idea. It was risky. If I hated it, it would be another thing to quit. But I smiled at the idea of building an inventory of things to talk about in my old lady years. Better to have tried and have an opinion rather than regrets.

"Do it. I support whatever you want to do," Jeff said.

And now that I had said it, I would have to do it. That was my way; if I verbalized it then it became my commitment to myself. My dad's voice echoed in my head: "Do what you say you are going to do. That's all there is to it."

The familiar process of re-verifying personal information began as soon as the anesthesiologist appeared. It was close to go time. The anesthesiologist completed his tasks, briefed Jeff on the drugging procedure, what to expect, and then left.

"You'll be pooping on the toilet in no time," I joked.

Jeff smiled. I always pushed him just a bit further into these personal matters than he would have gone on his own. But humor was my way to release tension.

The nurse appeared. "Ready?" she asked.

"Ready," Jeff responded.

I inhaled, letting my breath draw up the corners of my mouth for my best smile. I kissed him. "I love you," I said.

"Love you, too," said Jeff, and then he was off to the races. We separated and I walked down the blue and white corridor--the floors were always shiny. I rounded the familiar corner leading to the waiting area, déjà vu and dread seeping into my chest. I slowed my walking and paused just before entering the waiting area. I didn't want to be here again. I pushed the door open, and there were Joe and Sylvie. All I could think was *thank you.*

25| december 2016

I rode the familiar hospital elevator back to the second floor; the same floor Jeff had been on nine months ago. This time was different. I had pre-arranged childcare and this would be the finish line.

Next to Jeff's hospital bed in his new room was the metal visitor chair with the blue vinyl seat. *My seat,* I thought and took up my post in the chair. Jeff was still sleeping. The room was familiar in the sterile way doctor offices had become to me--devoid of emotion, which always struck me as odd since they were the places that housed so much emotion. The humming and beeping sounds of the hospital machinery faded into the background as I meandered through my thoughts.

Finally, I thought, we can get back on track as a couple and as a family. I will make every day count, take some time to get my head back in the game, and this will be a fresh start. Thank God. I had, after all, made a promise to God in this very hospital that if He would give us more time, I would make sure we lived our best lives. Now I had to hold up my end of the bargain. Jeff stirred. His eyes fluttered.

"Hey," he smiled.

"Hey, you're free," I said, leaning in to kiss his forehead.

"I am," he said with a smile and glanced down at his stomach where the colostomy bag used to be.

"Are you sore?" I asked.

"A little," Jeff said.

I knew if he admitted to being sore then he must be hurting. Just then a nurse popped in. "You're awake, how are you feeling?" she asked.

"Okay," he said.

I interjected. "Actually, he said he's a little sore." It was out of my mouth before I could consider if it was a good idea to speak on his behalf or not. The nurse looked at me with a smile that understood, She'd dealt with anxious wives before.

"A little sore is normal at first. Let me take a look at the last time you had something." She turned her attention to the monitor next to his bed. I flashed a quick look at Jeff and he smiled. Jeff knew I was nervous. I hated this powerless feeling. My phone binged with a text from one of our neighbors. The text was an invite to a neighborhood holiday party. This struck me as incredibly thoughtful as we didn't really know anyone in the neighborhood. After the initial polite welcoming this past summer, our lives took over, and I hadn't given much thought to anything beyond that. There had been a couple invites by some of the neighbors here and there, but the timing never worked out, and the truth was, I was uncomfortable. My regular dance of fitting in had grown more difficult these past few months.

I wished I could be a great neighbor like the ones my mom talked about having in Tennessee. The problem was, I always started planning out the conversation in my head before I even responded to an invite. All the fine print that came with my life would sound off and exhaustion would take over. I thought Wyatt's autism was an unavoidable topic as many of the kids in the neighborhood were Wyatt's age and they all went to the same school.

How's Wyatt?

Well, he has no friends and our life is one therapy session after the next, so, no we don't play rec basketball. We do speech, social skills, and OT. My husband had cancer and I'm stuck in this intersection of bullshit anger and fear. My career, um, used to be something to be proud of, but now I'm a quitter again. No, I don't know what I'm going to do next. No, I'm not teaching yoga--I quit that, too.

Good God! I had to stop the victim narrative, but I couldn't because it rang so loudly in my head.

The holiday party wasn't going to work anyway, as Jeff would just be getting home from the hospital. I declined the invite with a brief line explaining Jeff had just had surgery.

A few days later, we were all home on Sunday and my mother-in-law was coming by to pick up Wyatt for the day. Sylvie was helping Jeff and me by giving us some Wyatt relief. I would be able to take care of Jeff and have some quiet time for myself. It was an indulgence, like I was sick, too, but Jeff convinced me I should let his mom help. He was right; I was running on fumes and my shoulder pain would not let up. This new pain had developed over the past few months. My age was catching up with me or maybe the stress was. I figured a little home yoga practice might help.

The house was quiet. Wyatt was gone and Jeff was sleeping. In the family room, I slid the large wooden coffee table out of the way, rolled out my yoga mat, and launched a yoga class from my Cody app. Through yoga, I had learned to love being in my body. I found a way through movement and breath to get out of my head and move into my heart. I missed my yoga practice. I used to practice a few days a week. Yoga was my life, or at least reminded me how to be in and feel my life. There had been a time when I could be in a studio or in the company of hundreds of others practicing and still feel grounded. Now, even alone in my home, I searched for that same feeling.

My introduction to yoga was not love at first class. I had dropped into some Baptiste yoga classes here and there with Paige back in our late twenties. It served as the occasional stretch to counter all the cycling I was doing, which at its height, was easily a hundred miles a week. I didn't love yoga as the room was well over 100 degrees and often, someone would be sweating on my mat because their mat was two inches from mine, or a sweaty shoulder would rub against mine in the hallway coming and going into class. Gross didn't even cover how I felt about the yoga community. This was well before Lululemon invaded yoga studios and yoga mats became a yogi's personal runway for their latest athleisure wear, all while effortlessly striking Warrior Two.

My second tour with yoga was different. Post-Wyatt, workouts of any sort, especially biking, were a memory. I had tried to join the P90X movement. That failed as Tony Horton was not my cup of tea. In 2013, my neurologist suggested I take up yoga to help my migraines, which had gone from occasional to weekly. I was armed with new meds, a daily anti-seizure medication, and yoga and meditation was all he could offer.

There was a little yoga studio I noticed near my house back then called Studio 191. I was skeptical.

I was off on Fridays, which were my "me" days, a mix of errands and appointments. This particular Friday would be my "give yoga another shot" day. I pulled on my old, dated workout clothes, grabbed a yoga mat, and went to class.

Studio 191 was suburban cute, located in the back of a brown, seventies-styled, single-level office building. Inside, it had the requisite yoga mantras hanging on small, reclaimed-wood signs. It was clean and spacious with plenty of room to get in and out without random people bumping their sweaty bodies into mine. This made me happy. The teacher checking everyone in, Anthony, was younger than me. I wasn't expecting an old Indian guru, just someone who looked older than twenty-five. I wondered how much he knew about yoga. I had been to "gym yoga," and I really hoped this was not that. The studio was a nice shade of green, which was my favorite color so I decided that could be a good sign. The studio was hot, not Baptiste hot, but a thin layer of sweat was already forming on my forehead before my mat had been fully unrolled. The women in the studio all looked to be my age or older, fit and sporting some serious head-to-toe Lululemon--headbands, too. I laid down on my old mat, trying to ignore my frumpy workout clothes, and closed my eyes. Krishna Das was on and "Ma Durga" wafted softly through the studio.

Anthony walked in, adjusted the volume on the music, and began class. He left the music on, which meant I might not hear any of the potential loud breathers. I never really understood why people had to breathe so loudly in yoga. Baptiste yoga had their fair share of crazy breathers. It sounded like a Darth Vader-in-training conference some days. My other puzzling experience was the om-ing. The teacher would say five rounds of *oms*, but sure as shit, it would turn into this om-off and these crazy yogis would be om-ing loud and proud, going for gold—*for like five minutes!* This was not Baptiste yoga. There was no om-ing competition and I liked it already.

Anthony mostly taught in Sanskrit, so I had no clue what the hell he was saying. I craned my neck to look at other people who apparently knew the secret language of the suburban studio. Some of the words were vaguely familiar. I struggled with left and right, and Anthony quietly whispered in my ear "other right." At one point, I wondered if it was possible to drown myself in standing split as a steady stream of sweat poured into my nose. To say I was bad would have been a compliment. And the class was great. I had been out of my head for an hour and a half. I was horrible at this new version of yoga, but at the same time, I was inspired by it. I decided this was for me.

Every Friday morning after Wyatt got off to school, I made my way to Anthony's class, rolled out my yoga mat at Studio 191, and prepared to sweat my ass off. I was humbled to be taught by an amazing, young teacher. Eventually, I joined the league of Lulu and bought new yoga pants, strappy tops, and the headbands, too.

A year-and-a-half, hundreds of hours of classes, and many workshops later, I became a certified yoga teacher. In the process, a few pieces of my armor started to loosen. I noticed some of the stuff I had neatly packed away in closets and shoved down deep were starting to crumble. I was finding my "unrest"--as I had always called it--had a voice and needed to be worked out.

***

I finished my home yoga practice, switched off my TV, and sat in meditation, listening to the soft, mind-quieting handpan melodies of Kate Stone. The soft, ethereal drumming had a way of levitating my soul. When it was over, I told myself again, *life will continue, and it will be better. New.* I needed to reconnect with Jeff and Wyatt. I wanted to be happy and find my rhythm in the rush of life again. I had to stop waiting for the other shoe to drop. Waiting did me no good.

I got up, walked down the hall, and I noticed through one of the side windows flanking the front door a holiday balloon gently bobbing and swaying. I pulled open the door and a cold rush of air greeted my body. There on the front porch was a brown basket with a balloon tied to its handle. I looked around but the street was empty. I carried the basket inside thinking, *Oh God, how embarrassing. Whoever dropped this off had most certainly witnessed my yoga practice.* In the kitchen, I opened the basket, and a card revealed my neighbors had come together to compile a care package of various treats, homemade food, and--most adorable of all--"reindeer food" for Wyatt to leave out so that Santa's reindeers would not miss our house. These were the moments I had never been good at, receiving unexpected kindness and generosity. Becoming weepy over a basket of food and a helium balloon didn't seem rational, but what did anymore? How come it was always easier for me to put up a big wall and let someone yell at me or treat me badly than it was to accept generosity? I wiped my eyes and pulled a plate of food together for Jeff and arranged it neatly on a tray. He'd be touched by our neighbors as well.

***

As the preamble to Christmas, the early days of December also held the typical excitement of what Santa might bring. Wyatt was all in on Santa and his list had been locked and loaded. We had created a visual list, spelling and handwriting was still a challenge, so pictures of all the things Wyatt wanted, big and small, had been printed, cut out, and pasted to a poster board where a Christmas tree had been outlined in green tape.

Last January, while we were still living in the cramped apartment, I had packed away Wyatt's collection of Thomas the Trains, tenders, tracks, Cranky, Tidmouth Shed, and various other Thomas structures. Wyatt had not touched his trains for months and I knew how fickle kids were with their toys, so I waited for a couple of months, and still, Wyatt had shown no interest in his trains. The trains were packed up into large Rubbermaid storage bins and pushed under his play table and some went into my closet. We had a serious inventory and it was taking up serious space in a seriously small apartment.

Finally, a couple of months later, I decided it was time. I texted my friend Jill who had a little boy a few years younger than Wyatt. Tommy still loved Thomas Trains.

Me: Jill, would Tommy like our Thomas the Train stuff? Wyatt doesn't play with them anymore.

Jill was concerned. Was Wyatt really done with the trains? I assured her they had not come out in months; he was not interested. The trains were packed up, and as luck would have it, the next day in the school pick-up line, I pulled in behind Jill's minivan. Jill opened the back of her van and I deposited the trains into her car.

Maybe two weeks later, Wyatt asked, "Mom, where are my trains?"

I looked at Jeff for support, but he just shared my wide-eyed look of *oh shit*. My mind raced and then I had an idea, a story.

"So, you know how we just had Christmas and you just got all these new toys?" I asked, trying to sound upbeat and positive.

"Yes," Wyatt said in the trusting way kids do, probably in the way Hansel and Gretel took candy from the old witch in the woods.

"Well, Santa had to make room for the new toys, so he took away all the old toys you weren't playing with." Just as I was thinking my story wasn't half bad, Wyatt's expression revealed complete horror.

"*What?* Why would he do that?" Wyatt asked in disbelief.

"Honey, it's okay. Remember you just got all these really great new toys," I said, panicking silently. I had been wrong; the phase wasn't over.

"Call him! Call him right now! I want my trains back!" Wyatt insisted, his eyes were tear rimmed and the downturn of his mouth was heartbreaking. Jeff gave me a helpless shrug. I went to my bedroom and dug into my closet. I had saved a few of his favorite trains as keepsakes. I pulled them out, but Wyatt had gone into his room to lay on his bed to cry.

"You need to fix this. We can't have him hating Santa," said Jeff.

"I know, but I gave them to Jill for Tommy. We can't take them back," I said. "What do you want me to do, rebuy them all?" I asked in desperation.

"Yeah, if we need to," Jeff said.

I went into Wyatt's room; he was curled up on his bed staring off at the far wall. The far wall had been decorated with the story of *The Very Hungry Caterpillar*, by Eric Carle, which was one of his favorite stories. I sat on his bed, "Bug, I have an idea," I said.

"What?" he sniffed.

"Let's write a letter to Santa. He might not have all the trains anymore because he likes to help children who don't have toys, and he may have given them away, but let's write a letter and we'll see what Santa still has that he can send back to you, and whatever he doesn't have Mommy and Daddy will get you again. Okay?" I asked. Wyatt looked at me with hope and agreement.

"Tracks, too?" Wyatt asked tearily.

"Tracks, too," I agreed.

A letter was written to Santa and I began the process of scouring Amazon and eBay to restore the train collection to satisfaction. Jeff even ordered one train from a random eBay seller in Hong Kong. I filed this train adventure under life lessons.

I could not shake the guilt from the piece of bad fiction I had manufactured about Santa last year. As a result, I was compelled to tick off every item on Wyatt's list. I had to ensure Santa was really back in Wyatt's good graces because I had put him in the doghouse by mistake.

Christmas purchases from Amazon and Toys 'R' Us arrived almost daily. Meanwhile, Jeff healed, and I wrapped all the gifts knowing this was likely a chapter in "How to Ruin Your Kid 101."

Christmas morning came early. The sun was not yet up, but Wyatt was. Jeff successfully held him off, giving me time to hurry downstairs to turn on the Christmas tree lights, just like my mom had done when I was a kid. I plugged in the lights and took a step back. It was magic--the white glow of the lights on our first Christmas tree in the new home. The whole area was noticeably vacant of Wyatt's usual mess of toys because he had picked them up and "hidden" them from Santa the night before.

"Wyatt, come on down. I think Santa might have come and left you something," I yelled up the stairs. Wyatt sped down the hardwood stairs like a roll of thunder and in a blur of ripped paper, he conquered the days of wrapping I had labored over in what seemed like minutes. We had set up the fake Christmas tree in the corner of the breakfast room off the kitchen. This room was being used as a sitting area as we had foregone a kitchen table and mostly lived life at the island. The breakfast room was an open extension of the kitchen, all windows and a fireplace with two reading chairs. I loved this space for morning coffee, but today, in the sea of discarded paper, Wyatt was in his glory. I started to let go of some of my contempt for the house; it was becoming our home.

Jeff and I called this Christmas number one as we still had Christmas number two later at his parents' home. I loved our cozy Christmas with the three of us, small and intimate. The anticipation for Christmas had not resonated with Wyatt until the last couple of years, and now it was getting fun. The rituals of building up to the day, decorating, and reading Christmas stories were finally becoming our rituals, too. Wyatt's sense of time was not the same as other kids. When Wyatt began to anticipate Christmas, we knew this marked progress. Jeff and I happily focused on Wyatt's every reaction. I was so grateful for this Christmas together; we had earned it. I thought I saw the same feeling on Jeff's face, but it was hard to know. His smiles these days reminded me of how he used to embrace me when we first started dating--polite and tentative, like he was afraid of revealing too much. I remember finally saying, "Hug me like you mean it!" And then one day, he did.

Christmas at the Blaesers was no ordinary Christmas with Grandma and Grandpa, six married children of their own, and thirteen grandchildren. I had been to at least twelve Christmases with the Blaeser family, so it's not to say I was used to it, but *prepared* was a better word. Grandma and Grandpa didn't mess around either. Gifts were often large scale: iPads, gaming consoles, etc. This was a vastly different experience than my upbringing. In the beginning, it was overwhelming and difficult to digest.

The first time I met the Blaesers was Easter, 2003. Jeff had casually asked me if I had plans for Easter.

"Nope," I said.

"Would you like to come with me to my parents?" he had asked.

Of course! I wanted to meet his family—we had been dating on and off for a year, so this would finally mean we were dating for real.

His parents lived forty-five minutes north of Boston. Jeff picked me up Easter morning. I had bought a bouquet of mixed tulips for his mom the day before. The drive up was comfortable, and the conversation flowed like a typical day for us. I hadn't felt nervous until we pulled down the driveway. It wasn't a regular driveway. It could have been a road. His parents' home came into view as we wound down the drive, surrounded by a perfectly manicured lawn. The house emerged, giant, modern, and with a bit of a nod to something that Frank Lloyd Wright would have approved of. The oversized front doors were inset with a large carving of the sun.

As a teenager, my friends and I would drive to the beach through very wealthy parts of lower Fairfield County. Those homes had the most ostentatious doors and front walkways, and I always wondered who lived in those kinds of houses. The answer, so many years later, was about to be revealed to me.

Jeff pushed one of the heavy doors open for me to walk through first. On the other side was a spacious foyer, a soaring ceiling, and a marble floor. I felt small and even Jeff who stood over six feet tall seemed shorter in this house. I smelled the food first; tendrils of aroma woke up my stomach--Easter dinner. The smells were rich and homey, in contrast to the imposing foyer. I heard voices coming from further inside the house.

"Hello!" a female voice called. From the pitch and tone I

guessed his mother. Seconds later Sylvie Blaeser appeared in a doorway, all smiles and excitement. She had a warmth about her that also stood in contrast to the large foyer. Jeff hugged and kissed his mother and then introduced me.

We had been the last to arrive. All of Jeff's siblings and their spouses or significant others were already milling about the house or cozied into conversation as they sat casually on the ledge of the indoor koi fishpond. Sylvie and Joe Blaeser had a beautiful home, contemporary and *almost* imposing, except for the occupants who made it into a warm home. Jeff's family were really nice people, not polite in the way you tolerate a guest, but actually nice. My future brother-in-law, Matthew, married to Jeff's sister, seemed to know something I didn't. We had been standing off to the side in the dining room, near the buffet of desserts.

"This is an amazing family to be part of, honestly. You're going to love them!" Matthew beamed. Matthew and Leigh had married earlier that year. I attributed some of his enthusiasm to newlywed glow.

"Yes, everyone seems really nice--genuinely nice," I added.

"Oh yeah, they are--and it's real. It's exactly as you see it. I'm so lucky!" Matthew said.

It was weird to be having this conversation with Matthew. I really didn't know him, and Jeff and I were only recently established as boyfriend and girlfriend. *Part of the family* was a pretty big leap.

After years of dating, marriage, and having Wyatt, Joe and Sylvie's home was my home, too. The Blaesers were far from ostentatious. The immense sense of love and life that lived on the other side of the doors always drew me in the way a casual conversation might. Their home was always occupied with grandchildren, chatter, laughter and the busy noise of toys and TV.

"Merry Christmas!" Sylvie shouted happily from the kitchen

as soon as we entered. Wyatt kicked off his shoes and tore through the foyer, making a beeline for the living room where the presents and cousins were.

"Wyatt!" the cousins shouted. Wyatt always received a greeting meant for a king when he entered a room full of his cousins.

My father-in-law appeared first. "Merry Christmas and happy birthday," I said as I hugged him.

"Thank you, sweetheart," my father-in-law smiled and hugged me back.

"Best Christmas ever," my mother-in-law sang, gliding in from the kitchen to hug me. They were both full of love, polished with charm, and always willing to extend themselves to ensure you knew you had arrived at a place of warmth.

I suspected, in their active parenting days, the Blaesers had run a tight ship raising six children. There was no confusion where they stood on academics and athletics. Their children had a monopoly on attendance in the Ivies, and all of them had been athletes. I would often joke to Jeff that his family was the Blaeser Corporation with its own culture and way of being.

The Blaesers accepted me easily, as far as I knew. I made Jeff promise early on not to tell me anything bad his family said about me unless he thought it was something I would really want to know or should address. I was not perfect, and I knew they would, in time, see my imperfections, but in-law drama was not something I wanted. Besides, I liked liking the Blaesers and giving fuel to insecurities seemed like a foolish life sentence when it came to in-laws.

In the massive living room, the fireplace was blazing and the kids were circling the tall Christmas tree with its sea of presents. The presents had exploded all over the room, under the tree, on window seats, and ledges. *Overwhelming abundance,* I always thought. Leaning into Jeff, I said, "We'll never be able to compete with this."

The rest of the day was a montage of food, presents, and kids playing. No one talked directly about the year we had all just endured, and this included talking about Rachel—Jeff's younger sister who had also been screened for colon cancer as a consequence of Jeff's cancer. In fact, all of his siblings were advised to be screened once Jeff's cancer had been found. But Rachel, who ironically has the same birthday as Jeff, had a large precancerous tumor found and removed from her large intestine. I knew this had been a scary and jilting thing for her family, too. I remembered the long embrace her mother-in-law had given me in solidarity. "Thank God Rachel and Jeff will be fine," she whispered heavily into my ear, leaving traces of an emotional weight I understood, as we held each other tight.

At various time throughout the day, I noticed Sylvie beaming at Jeff with a mother's love. She would notice me seeing her and we'd connect in shared looks of gratitude and relief. Our prayers had been answered. This was typical Blaeser acknowledgment of what was difficult. Blaeser Corporation was tough and persevered. Onward and upward.

26| january – may 2017

January marked the start of my Introduction to Interior Architecture class. I kept my word to myself and started at the Boston Architectural College and I loved it. By the end of January, Jeff was on the mend from surgery and his life had seemingly picked back up where he left off. He was back to a regular work pace and his hair had grown back, nice and full.

But by the end of February, I was sure interior architecture was a passion and not a career-driven interest for me. The realization was a little deflating, even though I was telling everyone and occasionally myself that I was only interested in this to fill time. Deep down, I knew I needed direction. I had been quietly hanging my hopes on this for a bit of inspiration.

I reflected on my old career. Something about being in a corporate environment again didn't sit right with me. I had only left my job a few months ago, but it felt longer and less accessible. I was almost halfway through the semester and I decided to just finish it, commit, and be glad for the curiosity. I liked the technical aspects of what I was learning and the design components were fun. I loved being able to exercise my creative mind and it was invigorating to sit in a classroom again, even if I was the second oldest in the room. My classmates and even my teachers were young. I loved their passion and interest in the possibilities they imagined. I wanted to tell each of them, *Yes, do whatever drives your passion. Don't, under any circumstances, give it up because once you do, life has a way of piling bullshit on top of it and finding it again is hard work.*

In between learning how to draw plans, follow American with Disabilities Act (ADA) compliance, and learn color palettes, my friend David re-sparked the inspiration in me to write. It was not that I had been a writer, per se, but I had always written for myself privately, in between journaling.

David had worked on one of my teams years ago and had reached out looking for mentoring support. When we reconnected, I was honored to be thought of, considering we no longer worked at the same organization. David quickly became a good friend. He had re-appeared in my life when Jeff was first diagnosed with cancer. David's support was unexpected. I thought I was supposed to be supporting him, but he faithfully checked in to see how I was doing and how Jeff was doing. This simple act of consistently reaching out was just the right amount of support I needed.

Recently, David had started a blog and reading his writing reminded me how I once enjoyed writing. I had been writing since the seventh grade, little short stories here and there, but I never wrote anything to completion or shared. I still had my first green, faux-leather journal. I was inspired, so I started an anonymous blog. I was not as brave as David. My fear of sucking ended up not mattering because--if traffic were an indicator of success--it was a non-starter. But I loved writing, so I kept doing it. I had a lot of shit on my mind and opinions, and I lost myself in writing.

Jeff encouraged me. "Write. You're a great writer."

I brushed it off, rolling my eyes. "You say I'm great at everything." He was the opposite of my parents growing up who were a mix of cautious and never getting too proud. I didn't have an efficient processing system for accolades. Each piece I wrote, I shared with Jeff. I wanted another set of eyes to tell me if I was way off base. Sparks of re-connection with Jeff fired off in sputters as he read my pieces. It allowed him access to the inner parts of me. I began to inventory, however, all the ways I was opening myself to him, sharing my most vulnerable parts over the years, and still he wasn't opening up to me. I felt naked in my vulnerability, while he was warm and cozy in a giant down parka of not sharing.

I decided I would write a book about the challenges of our past year, but I stopped after two pages. The story was stuck because the shitty year, in truth, hadn't ended just because the calendar year had. We were still in it.

I tried to return to yoga, but was road blocked by my shoulder pain. After a number of doctor appointments and scans, I learned I had a partially torn rotator cuff. I repeatedly failed at modifying my yoga practice because my ego would not respect my physical limits. I was in pain most days and this did not improve my mood. *I used to be able to* . . . was my internal mantra. Three years ago, I had had labral repair surgery on my hip with a side of acetabulum reshaping, and in the past year, I was just getting back to running without pain. I wanted to be back to me. I was sick of life's speed bumps.

Jeff, meanwhile, was moving on with his life. He was fully immersed in work and not in me. He had restarted his life as if nothing happened. He wasn't seeing what the diversion had done to me.

We sat in bed one night talking about our growing distance and my unhappiness. I looked around our beautiful bedroom, it's high ceiling, chandelier, and fireplace. This room was the master bedroom of a happily married couple. We didn't fit in this picture. Our conversation was sad. I was sad. I didn't know how we ended up here.

"I support you. Do whatever you need to do to be happy," he repeated. I wondered why he thought he had nothing to do with my happiness. I paused to find my words.

"You shut me out for months--for the better part of a *year*. I get that you had to deal with your cancer in your own way, but you isolated me. I was just here, waiting and watching to see what was going to happen next," I said, holding back tears, but then I failed. A wet streak of tears rolled down my cheeks, and the caving in of my chest followed.

"I'm sorry. I didn't mean to," he said. "You know I love you."

I believed him. I knew Jeff was doing his best, but I still felt alone, and as quickly as my insides caved in, they rebuilt, hemming in all the hurt behind a protective shell of anger. I needed time to trust that if I leaned into him, he'd be there, like he used to be. This room, this house, this life, all of it was lonely.

"I know," was all I could say. I wanted to say, *I love you, too,* but the words were layers deep, buried under the weight of my sadness. I didn't know how to pry them free or to feel loved or loving at that moment.

***

The days continued, one weaving into the next, without any marking of progress except the passing dates on the calendar. I'm sure I *thought* I was good at hiding my growing apathy but maybe I wasn't at all. One day, I was talking to David on the phone when out of nowhere he suggested I read Mel Robbins' *The 5 Second Rule.* "It's a pretty good book," said David. "I think you'll like her."

Sure, I thought, *solve my life in five seconds.* For as often as David and I connected and talked about what was going on in his life, I was not willing to share how sad or lost I was feeling in my own. David was like my brother, living his sunny life in California. I liked *not* talking about me; it was like taking a vacation in his happy, transformative life. David had gone headfirst into transforming himself since moving out west. A week later, he sent me a link to a podcast to listen to of Mel Robbins. He must have known I hadn't taken his book recommendation to heart. I listened to the fifteen-minute podcast about rewiring your brain, and it spoke directly to me. I immediately downloaded her book, *The 5 Second Rule*, and I loved it.

"Mel is no bullshit. She has strength and she knows what it's like to skin your knees a few times. I like her," I told David. I imagined he was probably smirking on the other end of the line thinking, *Yeah, I told you so*. Next, David recommended *The Miracle Morning*. This time I took him at his word, no proof needed. I liked this book less, but I adopted and fell in love with the process it recommends. I created my own Miracle Morning routine, and every morning, as soon as I got Wyatt off to school and the house was quiet, I sat in one of my reading chairs in my office and meditated for the prescribed ten minutes. I found and created affirmations that served me. I visualized myself as a writer, got on my spin bike to exercise, and I read and journaled. Clarity flickered like little fireflies on a summer night.

Again, I returned to yoga despite my shoulder pain, but I couldn't settle in. Transitioning from one asana to the next, I felt stuck and clunky. I wasn't able to move my body like before. In every asana, I was anticipating the next--how would I modify to protect my shoulder? When I was in my body and moving fluidly, it had always stirred and then settled my emotions. Now, it was all stir without the settle. In savasana, I noticed how my yoga mat stuck to the backs of arms and back. I sensed everyone around me, including the loud breathers, and it annoyed me. I was aware of all the wrong things.

I needed the kind of clarity yoga used to bring me, like how it helped me find the quiet and grounding to know when I had to better connect to motherhood. But now my yoga mat was failing me; maybe I had used up all its magic.

April brought spring break and we were looking forward to another Blaeser family vacation. This year, we were off to Atlantis in the Bahamas. Wyatt was in his glory with his cousins. There was no better emotional and social support system in Wyatt's life than our family. It was also great timing as Wyatt had hit his annual I-hate-school time of the year, and school for Wyatt would continue through mid-August, so he had a ways to go.

Jeff and I slowed down and seemed to notice each other again in the Bahamas, despite the chaos of Atlantis where moms yelled about sunscreen--myself included--and the water generators were constantly roaring. Something told me the ancient Atlanteans, whoever they were, did not have the same ambient noise.

We found some quiet time on the balcony off our living room every morning and evening to admire the shades of pink and blue that streaked the sky and melted into the Caribbean Ocean. Even the peaks of the manufactured temples that rose above the transplanted Caribbean jungle added to the ambiance. Stealing moments in between taking care of Wyatt was always challenging, but on vacation, there were fewer distractions, so our moments together were a bit longer and more frequent. At home, I was guilty of allowing distractions to become commitments and priorities. Here, coffee together was a full cup and conversation, not just a few morning sips before Jeff was out the door. We could find our way back, I realized. We just had to take steps toward each other rather than around each other.

***

Back at home, mired in to-do lists and driving Wyatt from appointment to appointment, I wondered if Jeff and I had changed. We were looking at ten years of marriage this year, and even if the change was subtle, it could be enough to throw it all off balance. I wanted something more than an average life now. I wanted an extraordinary connection. If we were ever going to stare down the possibility of cancer or the like ever again, I wanted to feel gratitude for and confidence in having lived an amazing life. When I looked at Jeff, I saw a content person, but I didn't know what was inside.

When was the last time we had shared our dreams? I didn't think we wanted different things, but who knew? I hoped we were walking on parallel paths that just needed to merge again.

In writing, I found sparks of happiness that gradually moved me to a happier place. I continued with my Miracle Morning routine, which had started to give me the space within myself that my yoga practice once had provided and the inner quiet to look at all the messy bits stirring inside of me.

The adage "you are the company you keep" was not lost on me as David's willingness to open up about his own journey and transformation inspired me. The more he described his inward-looking process, the more curious I became about myself. In the past I had visited the island of self-reflection, but these visits were short, and their effects didn't seem to have a wide-sweeping impact on my day-to-day life.

A couple of years ago, my girlfriends and I attended a Bhakti retreat for a long weekend of yoga and meditation, hosted at a beautiful farm in upstate New York. We had been brought into this community by my friend Raghunath, an ex-monk and now master yoga teacher and spiritual mentor. The weekend was completely unplugged; no cell service, no TV or radio. While there was daily yoga, it was more self-guided meditation and reflection and sitting in sangha, which is community prayer, meditation, and discussion from excerpts of holy texts such as the *Bhagavad Gita* and the *Bhagavatam*.

The last day of the Bhakti weekend, everyone was sitting in sangha in an old barn. It was a beautiful August morning. Sun beamed through the open doors, warming the crisp air. Raghunath sat just behind his harmonium at the front of the barn with his eyes closed as he completed the last few notes of his soulful kirtan. He began his talk about labels, a simple concept, and a point of entry that everyone could connect to. He cautioned us to consider the labels we choose to put upon ourselves and the labels we allow others to put on us. I thought about this and the easy ones came first: not pretty, not smart, not a good enough mom, etc."

Raghunath shared his own labels that his parents had put on him, their impact, and the decision he made about himself. I considered this. What labels did I still carry from childhood, from others, and which ones had I given myself?

I closed my eyes and drew back the curtain in my mind, and I saw myself small and less than, in all the ways that had initially come to mind. But what came to me for the first time with clarity was the label *victim*. These incremental labels were summing up to *poor little victim*. And when something felt bad, I would justify it with self-deprecating talk—*I was weak, I was being stupid*. I was victimizing myself with shitty self-talk and words were powerful.

With my eyes still closed, I stayed alone with this realization. I began to witness all of its parts. I let the tears come. I had been victimized as a child—sexually abused--and I had long moved past the physicality of it, however, on this day, I was beginning to understand that the depth and impact of the trauma was more than that. It would be a couple years later before I finally unpacked all of its parts and moved past this. But on this day, as if standing at the bottom of a well, I began to see the clear blue sky above and climb toward it.

Raghunath talked about forgiveness for those who had put labels on us. I decided to start with me. I needed to forgive and love myself for every part of who I was. This was a pivotal moment for me. I saw myself as a little girl and I inhaled, exhaled, and quietly said to her, "Let it go. I forgive you. I forgive your anger." I knew I was not responsible for what had happened to me, but my anger had been so intense at times that for years it had been displaced. I was mad for so many reasons with one snowballing into the next, but mostly I was mad at myself. I had also been mad at my parents. I had always been at odds with myself over this. I didn't want to be mad at them but I didn't know how not to be. Logically, I knew what happened to me wasn't their fault, but if there was no anger then I'd feel sad. Sad always left me feeling weak and out of control. Anger felt powerful. But something beautiful happened that weekend being surrounded by a bunch of devotional bhaktis. I saw that anger was only an illusion of power. Victims were angry. I didn't need to be angry anymore—and there was no one to be mad at.

I was not being victimized anymore by anyone. And I would allow myself to be sad. Parts of my past were sad and always would be, but it did not have to always make me angry.

In moments like these, connection with myself and self-inquiry reconnected me to my joy. Releasing parts of my past was like finding new air. In my morning meditation, as I searched for connection with myself, I remembered Dhanurdhara Swami's writing that explains to be in service is to love and give and keep giving. He was another teacher I had looked to for spiritual wisdom. I had to remain in service and devoted to my marriage, despite my ego. When I was younger, I thought of devotion in terms of fidelity, but that was the easy stuff. Choosing devotion over the ego every day was the hard work.

Jeff and I kept trying to find things to talk about. In my mind, Jeff had more to discuss, but my days were boring. I did homework with Wyatt, drove him to therapies, and went to Whole Foods. I contributed little beyond the mundane tasks of my day. I was tired. My ego and victim story were in cahoots with each other and my internal battle to get back on track was making me emotionally black and blue.

One morning, Jeff left for work, leaving a trail of cologne behind him--the cologne Wyatt and I had picked out for him at Christmas. I assumed he didn't like it because he never wore it. My mind fired--an affair. I couldn't imagine him having an affair, but there was a part of me that reasoned, at this juncture, anyone would be more interesting and easier to deal with than me. Wasn't that why men had affairs--their wives were painful nags? And then there was that escapism component. What if he just wanted to get away from everything that reminded him of what he had just gone through? In my heart, I didn't actually feel it was a possibility, but my head could intellectualize it. I volleyed the idea around for a bit, trying to really imagine Jeff, his character, the person I knew, choosing this, as I swept the kitchen floor, unloaded the dishwasher, and slammed cabinets shut until I concluded that it didn't fit. I forced myself to put the idea away and remind myself 2017 was supposed to be our year. The year was not yet halfway through and there was still time and potential. Ideas like this were not going to help.

And so, I kept trying to connect with Jeff.

"What do you want me to do?" Jeff asked.

"How about you tell me what would make you happy?" I asked, trying to flip it around. I hated when he would ask that question, which put the pressure on me to come up with the big plan.

"I just want you to be happy," he said.

"You're kidding me," I said flatly. I wanted to yell at him. *No one is that selfless!* I was sure he was just trying to get out of expressing himself.

In truth, I wasn't doing a great job of expressing myself either. I didn't know how to tell Jeff how I felt or what I wanted. I had been saying the same thing over and over: "Tell me how you feel." Jeff heard my words as criticism and being told I was critical shut me down. I couldn't figure out what to say and how not to sound like an asshole. My heart, instead, retreated to the safer ground of silence and the sofa talks stopped.

In my silence, I became annoyed over everything. The things that used to slide started grating on me. Jeff drank too much beer, and every time I heard the crack of a beer opening, it echoed through my ears telling me that he did not care about his health. I was annoyed that he continued to eat junk food. I didn't like the way he did homework with Wyatt. His inconsistent approach created long tantrums from Wyatt before any work got done. I was growing so angry every day over everything and nothing.

I was leaving for England in a few weeks to visit some girlfriends for a little break that I hoped would help. One night before I left, I woke to the sound of Wyatt's sobbing. Jeff stirred a bit.

"I'll go," I said and hurried down the hall.

"Bug, Mommy's here. What is it?" I asked, climbing onto the top of the bunkbed with him and all his Mario and MineCraft stuffed animals.

"It was awful. I lost you," Wyatt sobbed.

It broke my heart to see and hear my little boy so sad. "Do you want to tell me about it?" I asked.

"No, Mommy. It was awful. I don't want to say it," he said through tears.

I hugged and snuggled him. "Bug, you're never going to lose me. I'm right here," I said, kissing his tear-streaked face.

The risk of the white lie set in almost immediately. What if something did happen when I was in England? Would he hate me forever rather than miss me? Weren't these the moments kids relived in therapy years later?

***

My visit to England was much needed "me time." I found some space to be with my own thoughts and connected with old friends. We ate good food, lost hours in good conversation, crossed the countryside in trains, and stayed in various places.

In the Lakes Region, the land romantically faded into the low-tide of the ocean, while at the Jurassic coast, exposed, stark white cliff sides crashed into vivid green grassy hilltops. At the base of the cliffs, waves caught on jagged edges creating a misty spray that veiled the entire landscape in a soft haze. I fell in love with the English countryside.

And finally, I stood before Stonehenge and its impressive stones, and I loved considering the riddle of how they got there. Like the Colosseum in Rome, however, it didn't feel as big to me as I thought it would. Was this also like my life--some stuff just felt bigger until I stood before it and stared it down? Sure, the stones were massive and heavy, but there were some good working theories that really broke the mystery down of how the site could have been built.

Over the years, I learned that getting out of my environment had this magical way of helping me regain perspective. Home easily became a vortex of distractions. Standing before man's great achievements, including some of the Seven Wonders, I always felt content with my place in the world. It was as if the universe whispered to me, "It's going to be fine. Everything is as it should be." I was inspired by the kaleidoscope of possibilities. I was comforted that there were and would continue to be greater things in this world than my life. My decisions good or bad were inconsequential in the scheme of things.

***

On my flight home, I revisited the beauty of everything I had experienced. I had always been so close to these beautiful places but had not ventured out of London before. It made me wonder what was I missing in my marriage that I was not venturing out of my comfort zone to see. The time away was a good reset. I missed Jeff and Wyatt.

Jeff and I found more contentment in our daily interactions. We were back to chatting about the day and its mundane happenings, but with less attitude and resentment on my part. I was trying again. Jeff would come through the door at 6:00 p.m., drop his belongings in the mudroom, find me, smile and ask, "How was your day?" It was a well-intentioned, innocent question, but one that I needed to take a deep breath before I could work through my answer. The problem was my days were lacking and generally uninspiring and putting words to this would make it real.

"Fine, how was yours?" I'd ask. We were existing fine, and I think we were both glad for the break in drama. We focused on Wyatt's summer and getting him ready for Whitman Summer Camp in August. We were unsure if Wyatt would be a fit for their program and if he would tolerate the full day out in the sun. Wyatt had somehow come to the conclusion that the sun made his hair grow, and therefore, he did not like to be in the sun because he didn't want long hair. I would have a couple months to build his sun-tolerance and get him excited for camp. In the meantime, I bought Wyatt a collection of various hats.

With the end of May, I completed my final project for my Interior Architecture class. The project was to design an entire space, floor to ceiling, and I loved my project. I presented my various drawings, elevations, electrical plans, color palette, and furnishings to my class. The presentation was fun. I had forgotten how much better I had gotten over the years at presenting. The class had been really enjoyable and scratched an itch of curiosity I had had, but it was not a calling. The idea of heading down a path toward another career that was not making an impact left me uninspired. After my presentation, I stacked my boards, tucked them away, and went back to writing.

27| june - december 2017

Summer was starting and my seasons had long been marked by the rhythms of Wyatt's school year. This was IEP approval time and it brought out the worst in me. On Facebook, moms were already posting about summer camps and last day of school parties. I scrolled past them with a quick flick of my index finger. I knew these posts were people's personal life advertising, or FaceBrags as I called them, but I wanted to belong to the effortless club. Despite being squarely invested in my life and loving my son and at the moment, pain-in-the-ass husband, I had days where I longed for effortless without having to sign off on yet another IEP. The pressure to ensure Wyatt's IEP was perfect could feel overwhelming.

Wyatt was in the extended year program, which the school recommended for any child in the special education program. Wyatt hated it, and I hated it for him. Summer school meant there was no natural end of school for him, save for the last two weeks of August.

This summer would be a little different. We'd kick it off with the cousins for another Blaeser family vacation and soon-to-be tradition on Lake Winnipesaukee in New Hampshire for the week of July fourth.

The week was fantastic. Sylvie had rented a house on the lake that was large enough to house most of the family. Jeremy and

Miranda, Jeff's brother and sister-in-law, and their four kids would be in their own summer house ten minutes away, which they had bought years ago. Each day, the entire family ate, swam, boated, and tubed together.

Being at the lake had an old-fashioned easiness to it. For the first time in a long time, we all stayed off of our iPads and iPhones, which were tucked away for the majority of the day. Evenings held an even more unexpected enjoyable experience for me--kitchen time, preparing dinner with my mother- and sisters-in-law. Women in the kitchen preparing dinner is not something I would typically have jumped on, but this was truly enjoyable. The time together was less about the food and entirely about the company. Sylvie and her daughters, Rachel and Leigh, were funny. They not only loved each other, but *liked* each other, which was not always a given in families. To be included felt special.

Throughout the week, one of my brother-in-laws mixed drinks, something summery with elderflower, and while I am not a drinker, a little here and there was nice. The kids played and occasionally picked up their summer reading books, which were littered about the house. This was a week of friend time for Wyatt, who considered his cousins to be his best friends. Nothing makes my heart more full of love and admiration than watching the way my nieces and nephews interact with Wyatt. They hold him high, and despite knowing Wyatt is on the spectrum, they don't give him special privileges. Wyatt is a normal kid with them. They never disregard him. They make him work to be understood or work to keep up. They are a team, and perhaps it's a byproduct of them all being little athletes, but they encourage and cheer for his progress and accomplishments. They have been able to get him to do things because of their sheer excitement that no one has been able to. Wyatt has always been a water bug but getting him to swim and not look like he's drowning, well, that has been a challenge. Enter my superstar niece, Polly, who can outswim most girls her age throughout the state, add a race with the boy cousins, some cheering, plus a head start for Wyatt, and like magic, we have a swimmer's stroke!

My nieces and nephews remind me Wyatt is more capable than my parental-fear allows me to believe at times. This is the superpower of Blaeser Corporation, I tease Jeff, but I am eternally grateful for it.

Jeff and I were relaxed and content with each other around his family. The distraction of our disconnection was put aside for the time being. The full house of adults offered me the chance to run in the mornings and start the day with a clear head. My shoulder was officially shot, further confirmed a few weeks earlier by a second opinion that I had torn my rotator cuff. Yoga was out but running was still a way to quiet the crazy in my mind.

The roads around the lake were shaded and hilly, just the way I liked my runs to be. I like a long, smooth run up a hill. It was the same when I biked. Breathe, focus, and move. When I got back to the house after a run one morning, my left knee was throbbing with sharp pains. I was annoyed and I told Jeff. We both knew when my body started to signal pain it was generally no good. Despite the early warning, I continued to run throughout the week. I was greedy for the mental benefits.

When we returned home I made a physical therapy appointment with my regular guy, John, to look at my knee. He had helped me with my hip and ankle and was working on my shoulder. I went to appointment after appointment, including acupuncture, but nothing helped. I had put yoga on hold and now running and biking were out until the pain stopped.

***

As the summer progressed, I was aware that the mini-session at Whitman Summer Camp was approaching. I had signed Wyatt up early in the spring for Whitman Summer Camp. When Whitman accepted him, I was literally teary with joy. Other camps did not accept a child on the spectrum, but Whitman was willing to give Wyatt a chance. Then before camp could fail, I panicked and pulled the ripcord.

"We're not going," I told Jeff. "I just can't do it. I'm too nervous and I think he's going to be miserable."

"Are you sure?" Jeff asked.

"Yes. What happens when the kids are mean to him? Or if the camp counselors can't manage him when he has a meltdown about not wanting to do something? Like being in the sun too long?" I asked.

"Okay, not this year then," Jeff said. I could tell he was sympathetic to my worry.

"Do you think your parents will think I suck?" I asked, realizing my own defeat.

"No, not at all. Don't worry about them. I'll talk to them. Has my mom said anything to you?" Jeff asked.

"No, I just know that she would like to see Wyatt in something. I mean, I would too, but it's just so damn hard. No one would take him and I just don't think this is going to work."

"I know, it's okay. You do a great job with Wyatt. Everyone knows that. You worry too much," Jeff said.

I was miserable with worry. Wyatt's language was still behind and he never really told me things until well after the fact. I could not stomach the idea of kids being mean to him and Wyatt lacking the language to advocate for himself. *How would I know if something happened to him?* This camp was not set up for special needs kids, as they had been keen to emphasize to me. I wondered how they would handle other children being unkind. I had never been able to forget the situation Kathryn, Wyatt's first nanny, had encountered with him a few years ago when some kids had been encouraging him to play ball with them. They would throw the ball toward him only for another boy to intentionally take it, never letting Wyatt actually join in and play.

I had once witnessed some boys at the local park not letting Wyatt play with them and I heard one saying he was going to "punch him in the face if he didn't go away because he was the slow kid." These memories colored my judgment and were perhaps a similar shade of my own memories of being teased as a child for being Korean. I couldn't know for sure Wyatt would have an advocate at camp.

***

In the background of my life was the constant noise of hammering and sawing as we had decided to finish our basement, build a gym, an additional bathroom, and a secondary family room. Because of the continuous construction noise, I determined that there was no way I could do any writing or blogging. The next best thing for me would be to see what was on Netflix. I was injured and I couldn't run, bike, or go to yoga anymore. I had some time to kill before Wyatt was home from summer school, so why not catch up on some shows?

It started off innocently enough watching *13 Reasons Why* and then on to *Sense8*, *The Last Kingdom*, *Peaky Blinders*, and on and on, and before I knew it, I was in my Summer of Netflix binging. I watched everything. There is not much I couldn't talk fluently about when it came to Netflix shows. I even included some substance and watched *Auschwitz: The Nazis and the Final Solution,* which was horrifying and may have contributed to some horribly depressing days. Then one day, I watched the entire docuseries *The Defiant Ones* over a full pie. In the recesses of my mind I knew I was being a lazy ass. I felt a little embarrassed about the contractors working on the basement noticing that my TV was on all the time and I was parked in front of it. My sofa called episode after mindless episode, and I lost all thought of and motivation for a life outside of Netflix and trips to my pantry. I eventually ran out of new things and re-watched the full series of *Parenthood*. I became obsessed with the characters--the Bravermans were my people. I couldn't stop watching. It was as if I was watching a part of my life: I had an autistic child, my partner had cancer, we were one and the same. The more I watched it, the more I found myself falling in deep to my victim story from the past few years. I finally had something to share my feelings with, and it was giving back, episode after episode. It became my emotional connection. Like feeding myself a giant bag of candy, I was filling up on junk that wasn't real. I was eating actual junk, too. Three of four meals were Pringles with an occasional mix of cookies. The cookies were from the bins at Whole Foods, so how bad for me could they be? They became another form of comfort.

Occasionally, I came out of my Netflix haze and Jeff and I would have a surface-level, friendly conversation.

"How was your day?" Jeff would ask the standard greeting when he walked through the door.

"Fine" or "uneventful" I might say. I imagined Jeff steadying himself, then opening the door every night, knowing that he'd find me on the sofa watching *Parenthood* or making the same boring dinner, chicken with some vegetable. I wondered why we were so lost for words. I was tired of being the purveyor of conversation. It was time for Jeff to put in a little more effort, I thought, as the remote stayed within arm's distance from me at all times.

Last year had been our ten-year wedding anniversary, but with Jeff in chemo, we agreed we would table the ten-year anniversary trip. The ten-year anniversary trip was something we had dreamed up when we were first married. Our ten-year anniversary would be a capital 'A' amazing trip to celebrate the milestone.

One night, I was sitting on the sofa, finishing up an episode of *Parenthood* when Jeff came home from work. "How would you feel about going to Cairo? We haven't planned anything yet for the big anniversary trip," he said.

I perked up, reached for the nearby remote, and pressed pause. This question I liked! "Yes, definitely. When?" I asked. The Great Pyramid was on the list of Seven Wonders, which had become part of the bucket list I had been working on for a few years. The Great Pyramid would be number seven and qualified as an A-mazing trip!

"In two weeks. I was thinking we could go when Ben goes to visit with Kendall," Jeff said. I vaguely remembered that Ben, Jeff's brother, was going to visit his son, my nephew, in Egypt. Kendall had done a semester there and was staying on the summer to volunteer and teach English to refugees.

Two weeks from now? My heart sank. There was a snowball's chance in hell that I would be able to find childcare for Wyatt with such a short window, but I'd try. Meanwhile, I couldn't help but notice that this was Ben's trip and not actually ours, but I said screw it, it's Egypt. I fired off a few texts to sitters we trusted. While I waited for responses, I flipped open my MacBook. In no time, I found an Oberoi Resort that looked dream-like. I had discovered Oberoi Resorts while in India; they were palatial and luxurious with endless water features.

Unfortunately, none of our sitters were available. The pyramids were out. But since we were on the topic of the anniversary trip, we continued to think about what we should do. Next, I chased down Venice for early August, but again, childcare for a long enough time eluded us. We had no sitter for Wyatt. Asking my mother-in-law seemed selfish and too much for her. We would have to make do with what time we could get from Kathryn, who was able to give us four nights.

Jeff suggested Puerto Rico for the amount of time we had, so

I planned a trip to the Ritz Reserve Resort at El Dorado. The resort was built into the forest with a minimal footprint. The rooms all had open-air options, plunge pools with beautiful views of the ocean, and acres of paths for hiking and biking. We had hoped that this time together would be good for us to reconnect. We knew it would take more than one trip to fix the divide that had been growing between us--we were not unrealistic in that way--but we knew we had to start somewhere. A quiet nature resort seemed like a great place to start.

Without the distractions of our everyday life, a familiar version of our old selves started to emerge again. The quiet easiness resurfaced, but I had become more private with my thoughts than I had been in years past. It was hard to keep giving and sharing myself emotionally and not receive the same openness in return. Jeff was always willing and flexible. When it came to activities he had always been up for following my lead, but now I was changing the expectations a bit. I wanted more.

In Puerto Rico, we relaxed into the lush environment, enjoyed the spa, biked, ate great food, and made love, but I didn't believe in those moments we were in love. We loved each other with devotion and gratitude, but where did my best friend go?

I wondered if Jeff thought the best version of himself was when he was doing what I wanted. In an old version of our relationship, that may have seemed great to me, but these days, I was tired of being in charge all the time.

We returned home rested and glad for the time together and the vacation glow lasted about a week. My Miracle Morning routine had disappeared entirely, along with my writing time. Once Wyatt returned to school, I vowed I would get back into a routine. Even as I thought this, I knew it was the same kind of talk I used to judge silently when I heard other people talk about getting healthy next month or at the start of the New Year. Why was I waiting?

As the summer wrapped up, flag football started, and I signed Wyatt up for two weeks through the town's Parks and Recreation department. I had called ahead, giving my speech about Wyatt being on the spectrum and how he may need extra support and encouragement. I was assured this was no problem. This would be an entirely new sport for him, but someone had mentioned the town program was great and would be a great way for Wyatt to begin to socialize with other kids. Another plus: it was in the early evening, so there was less hot sun for Wyatt to contend with. After my panic over Whitman Summer Camp, I felt like I owed him the chance.

We arrived at the packed field of kids and coaches. All of the other kids seemed to know each other or were with a sibling. I stayed with Wyatt until the kids were called into groups, as I would have rather cut off my arm than leave him standing alone. Finally, Wyatt and the rest of the kids were called into their respective age groups, and I took a seat in the stands with a parent I knew. It wasn't long before the mass of kids broke into lines for drills and there in the middle of the field was Wyatt, sitting by himself. Internally, I freaked out. *Don't they see my son? He's alone!* As I stood to go down to him on the field I heard another mom yell to her son, "Quinn, go make Wyatt feel comfortable!" it was Jeni from my neighborhood. Her son Quinn was in the older boys' group, but she had seen Wyatt, too.

"It's okay," I said, as I waved and hurried out onto the turf, my heart cracked open a little. It was the kindness from my neighbor, who I really didn't know, that did it. If I could have hugged Jeni I would have. As I made my way out to Wyatt I called Jeff on my cell. "You need to come here now! Wyatt is alone and no one is helping him and I don't know how to play football!" I said on the verge of tears. I sounded angry but I wasn't. I was sad and hurt for my son who had just been left behind. I made my way to Wyatt. By this time, he was sitting on the ground by himself.

"Hey Bug, want to join the other kids? I asked.

"No," he said.

"I know it's hard doing new stuff, but Dad is on his way, he is going to be your partner." I encouraged.

"Okay." Wyatt softly agreed, looking around for Jeff.

"It'll take a few minutes, but I'll stay with you," I said.

By this time, one of the coaches noticed us and had made his way over to encourage Wyatt to join the group, which Wyatt did. I wanted to yell at the coach and tell him he was a jerk for not noticing my kid earlier. But he wasn't, not really. I was feeling hurt for Wyatt. And I was mad at myself. I had created this situation. I had told him this would be fun.

Twenty minutes later Jeff showed up, strode out onto the field and partnered up with Wyatt. With his arrival I felt saved from this horrible situation I was failing at. Why didn't I know how to play football? I had freaked out and felt intimidated by all the male coaches on the field and shrunk. Flag football day one did not go well. Jeff tried his best to help Wyatt but there were too many rules for Wyatt to keep track of.

Before we finally put a pin in it, we had asked our nephews to play with Wyatt as maybe a less-intimidating preview would be helpful. One afternoon, Chase, Pete, and Nathan, Pete's friend, corralled Wyatt into the yard after swimming.

"Wyatt let's play football," Pete encouraged as he dumped the pouch of flags onto the ground. Wyatt looked down, threw his head back in protest,

"I hate fags!" he yelled in defiance.

Pete and Nathan, typical fourteen year old boys, tried to restrain their smirks. Wide eyed and horrified I fired a look to the boys, mouthing, "No." I guess pronouncing "L" was still giving Wyatt a hard time. But that was the truth--he didn't like flag football; it never took.

***

As another school year started, the routine began again with all its same monthly school meetings, doctor appointments, and therapy. Despite the renewed excitement fall typically brought for me with the anticipation of change, I felt nothing this year. I wanted to be excited about something, but I had nothing. I had no great inspiration. I was stuck. I wanted to be unstuck, but I didn't know in which direction to move first.

Instead, I fixated on Jeff and me. We were back to struggling to create a new love. I sensed Jeff looking to me for direction, but I didn't have it. I couldn't fault him. I had always taken up the role since the day I asked him out. I didn't know how to direct us. I didn't know how to direct me. I didn't love him less, I just didn't love the hand of cards we'd been playing.

And part of that was about me. I could not hold on to happy. Self-pity's siren call had me in its grasp again and I was binge-watching TV while sprawled on the sofa.

I found the show *The Vikings*. I should have maybe been motivated by their fierce, kick-ass attitude, but I wasn't. Mostly, I wondered how the hell they managed to survive the trip to England. I played it over and over in my head. Would I have sat under the tarp they fashioned as a tent on the boats and would that have been enough, or would I have been better off in the open air not getting seasick? I barely made the sail from Newport to Nantucket many years ago. I had made my boyfriend at the time leave his sailboat and we flew home at the close of the weekend.

Hadn't I once been someone fiercely independent, who lived on my own terms and waited for no one? Now, I focused on wondering if I were a Viking, where I would sit in the boat.

My email inbox filled daily with job posts from Indeed, and I considered if going back to work again was the answer. Jeff was healthy, so I could get a job. But I worried that if something happened again, I would just have to quit, which was more difficult than starting again.

"How was your day?" Jeff continued to ask.

"Fine," I would say, as if we were performing a call and response. Then one day, after my typical "fine" I said nothing else. I made no other efforts, didn't bring up any bullshit topics, I just closed down the conversation factory. We didn't speak until the next evening. We ate in silence and moved around each other as if we were strangers.

"Have I done something wrong?" Jeff asked the next evening.

"No," I said.

"Well, you aren't talking to me."

"I know, and you aren't talking to me. I guess I just wanted to see if you would initiate a conversation."

This kicked off a night of talking and borderline fighting. I was tired and wrong, I knew it, and I was acting passive aggressively. Even if I had been right, my behavior sure wasn't helping. I knew this, but it was like an itch my ego could not leave alone. It had to be scratched.

The next day, I considered the words of Dhanurdhara Swami while I was journaling. "Be equipoised, detached, not absorbed in my happiness, otherwise suffer." I needed to cut the shit and work on being less angry. I paused and sat in silence for a bit longer asking myself *why* to every answer I produced. I settled on realizing that I was afraid. I still held fear that I could lose Jeff. Another of Dhanurdhara Swami's writings came to me: "Pleasure will always be mixed with the fear of loss." This one seeped in more deeply.

It was still difficult for me to drive away from Northshore General Hospital without my heart racing and feeling short of breath after those horrifying days when Jeff was initially hospitalized. The uncertainty of those days had eroded me. The fear that I would lose him unraveled me as I gripped my steering wheel.

Why was it so hard to love in the way that I felt it? It was whole and pliable in my heart, but all my external expressions got caught in a kind of dirty dryer vent and the air was restricted. Nothing came out right.

***

"Wyatt, how was your day?" I asked, ironically aware I sounded like Jeff. I wondered if those words had the same effect on Wyatt as it did on me.

"Good," Wyatt said.

"What did you do?"

"Played links," he said.

"Who did you play with?" I asked.

"Myself." My heart sank. Why weren't the teachers helping him play with other kids? His paraprofessional aid was supposed to help support his social engagement. A sharp sadness sliced through my chest as I conjured visions of Wyatt being alone. I knew he needed to experience life on his own terms and create his own story, but right now he was still my baby and I wanted to run interference on bullshit like this. I was torn about what I should do. I knew this was life. There would be heroes and villains in his story, for sure. And eventually, he'd discover villains were not always played by people, but instead, by diseases like cancer. I set up a special email account for him a few years ago that I planned to someday give him access to. Someday, he'd read the email I sent him about when his dad had cancer. The emails would either give him a better understanding of his life or examples to bring into therapy.

A week later, rather than asking Wyatt day after day how his day was, I decided to practice telling him how my day was. I told him about the parts I liked the best and the parts that were the most difficult and we talked about his day in this way, too. While this tactic proved more fruitful, it didn't turn my son into an endless faucet of conversation. But I was happy for any new bit of information Wyatt was willing to share and every day I learned a little bit more. Wyatt was struggling at recess; it wasn't his favorite. Every day, my little boy stood by himself. This tore my heart apart in a million pieces. Had I done this? We had asked the school to retain Wyatt in the first grade, and now the boys he knew were a grade ahead of him and he did not recess with them. I opened my MacBook, fired off an email to his teacher and made a note to discuss this in our next monthly meeting. Guilt, responsibility, and blame had a cage fight in my mind for the night.

A month passed and I got back into my Miracle Morning routine. Being a creature of habit, the routine helped settle me and the intensity at which I was feeling pissed off dropped off a bit. I wrote in my journal: *I want change. I am everything I need to be. I have the ability already, be open to it.* If nothing was permanent then putting every bit of myself into disappointment, anger, or unhappiness was not serving me and never would.

***

Ben, Jeff's brother, was going to New York City to see Guns N' Roses in October. "Hey, want to go the GNR concert with Ben?" Jeff asked one night. Without hesitation, I answered, "Yes."

Guns N' Roses made me think of "Sweet Child O' Mine" and "Paradise City." "Paradise City" brought me back to a ski lift, queuing up the song on my Walkman for my reckless descent. I was not nearly as good a skier as everyone else, but I tried hard, and with Axl screaming in my headphones, I imagined I was the shit. "Sweet Child O' Mine" takes me to summer, watching the black and white music video on MTV. It was a time in my life when my peak desire was to be a white girl because they were the prettiest. They were the image of beautiful, sexy, and desirable in every

MTV video. I loved how the guitar opening in the song made me smile and consider life's awesome possibilities. I did that a lot as a teenager--anxiously awaited growing up. When I grew up, I thought, maybe I would be pretty.

At forty-five, I realized I had been pretty in my younger days but was so concerned about *trying* to be pretty that I missed seeing it. Now, I was a middle-aged-mom, finally going to a GNR concert with my husband. I wondered what would I see when I looked back fifteen years from now.

Going to New York for the concert was unexpected and a lot of fun--precisely what I needed. Ben had planned everything; the chartered plane, hotel, concert tickets, and even spa reservations. The weekend was effortless, and Jeff and I laughed, held hands, and found familiarity in each other's presence. I remembered this guy who made me laugh.

After dinner, the night before the concert, Jeff and I wandered around the meatpacking district and SoHo. I loved the city. I had so many memories of walking these same streets at various times in my life: clubbing, killing time before a Broadway show, shopping, and trying to feel part of something special. Tonight, holding hands with Jeff, we were in something special. Maybe it was the moment where we started to fall "in" love again or at least the moment we knew it wasn't lost.

***

The remainder of the year flew by. The holidays came fast. Wyatt drew up his list for Santa as I drew up my enormous to-do list. I loved and dreaded this time of year. Jeff's family, my family, schoolteachers, and specialists all needed gifts.

Around me, all the Christmas shone bright, but my internal light that had once been on was still only flickering. My morning meditations left me more perplexed than settled. Where had my faith in my self gone? Where had Jeff and I gone? Date nights were fine, but the magic faded too fast. Maybe the "we" was lost because my half was lost. Waiting for him to let me in was stupid. I had no control over him or "us" and waiting was killing me. These glimmers of hope and what felt like false starts were making my head and heart spin. It was time to get my heart and soul realigned. All this time I had been holding onto this promise of living *our* best life, but it was unrealistic. I only had control over *my* best life.

Bing! A text came in from Megan. I couldn't remember the last time I had heard from her--it had to have been over a year. Megan and I had worked together for five years building the operations teams at the software consulting firm and had become close during that time.

Megan: Can you talk on Sunday at 3pm?

Me: Yes

I wondered if everything was okay, but Sunday was just a few days away, so I'd find out soon enough.

Sunday afternoon rolled around, and the phone call with Megan was awkward. I found myself looking out the kitchen window, talking myself out of being annoyed, I wasn't in the mood for being sold.

"You should do this for yourself. You deserve to do something for you," Megan said. She was trying to get me to sign up right then and there for a week-long transformational workshop. It was the same workshop my friend David had done. The timing was right; I was already planning a trip out to California where the workshop would be hosted, but for some reason, I was compelled to dig in just a little bit. I was being stubborn even though I knew I was going to sign up. I had, in fact, decided a month ago that I would, but I didn't like being pushed and it was starting to piss me off.

Megan continued. "What's stopping you?" I wanted to yell

into the phone, *If you have to ask me that question then you really have no clue about my life.* And she didn't, at least not in the past couple years. I hated feeling like I was being challenged about my personal life in this way by someone who I thought didn't have a front row seat to it. What's stopping me? *Who will take care of all the shit that needs to happen every day? There is a whole lot of effort to make all this work; it's not easy! Of course, you wouldn't know that in your easy, single life!* I wanted to shout. Lately, I was aware most things pissed me off so I knew it wasn't Megan. By the end of the call, I signed up for the workshop. I decided to stop digging in for the sake of control.

I didn't know a lot about the workshop, but at the same time, I didn't care. If I hated it, I'd just leave and go back to my brother's house who I'd be out there visiting anyway. The cost was strangely cheap and just watching Netflix wasn't working that well for me as a transformation tactic—the Bravermans weren't real people!

My Summer of Netflix and Pringles had caught up with me. My reflection in the mirror might have been influenced by my emotional state, but my clothes didn't lie. They were slutty tight; even my yoga pants looked too small. I needed new clothes, but if I was going to buy clothes it wasn't going to be because I was too big for the ones I had. Something in me snapped. I didn't feel like me and now I didn't look like me. I made a decision and hired a nutritionist and an online fitness coach, Karen. My shoulder was still a mess, but it was time to move through my excuses. I was, after all, a trained yoga teacher, so I had a sense for anatomy and how to work through modifications for injuries. I had just been lazily licking my wounds for too long.

Karen, the nutritionist/trainer, wanted weekly pictures and stats sent to track my progress. This brand of accountability, I knew, was going to hurt my feelings, but I began to move in the basement that had been finished over the summer and now had a gym in it. Miracle Mornings plus workouts became my routine before the mindless daily to-dos. I put my butt on my spin bike, logged into my Peloton account, ate according to my defined macronutrients, and hit my calorie burn four times a week. I did this every week, February through June. Slowly but surely, my "Pringle suit" fell off and I started to feel better.

***

In February, Jeff and I went to Miami for a long, Wyatt-free weekend. The trip felt like being in New York again when parts of who we had been surfaced. *We really do like each other!* I wanted to shout, as we laughed, joked, and walked around holding hands. We stayed at the Standard South Beach hotel, subtitled "the adult playground," which became evident at the poolside amateur flesh-show. As we were checking out, a couple came in from partying all night wearing matching leather chaps. Maybe, I considered, the couple who wears leather chaps with their bare asses hanging out together, stays together.

Somewhere in the process of feeling physically better about myself, I stopped being so pouty all the time. In April, Jeff had to travel to Miami again for a business trip and he asked me to accompany him. The trip was less of a couple's getaway, but there were again slivers of us. I wondered what about getting away connected us? Were we like those people who are great in long distance relationships, but fall apart once they live together? Something about home and the bullshit that lived in the small spaces of our lives tripped us up.

***

Just before I left for California, a coach, A.J., called me to prepare me and do some intake for the transformational workshop. This was good because I still really had no specifics on what I had signed up for. A.J. gave me this word--*intimacy*--and a new way of thinking about the word, saying this is how he described the workshop. Intimacy *into-me-you-will-see.* Still not entirely clear on what that meant, I shrugged it off, but many weeks later, I got it.

***

May came quickly. I signed Wyatt up for a summer camp, this time for kids on the spectrum. It was a camp he had participated in years ago that would be easy. I wouldn't have to panic and pull him last minute. I was in California before I knew it. The visit with my brother and his family was perfect. I met my new nephew, who was adorable like all babies are. My brother and his wife were settling into parenthood well and I wondered what their lives would be like. When I observed my brother, I saw glimmers of my parents in him. Was that because he was their biological child? I always questioned what was learned or inherited. I remembered that time in mine and Jeff's life, when we had just started with Wyatt and it was all so new, fast, and exciting.

Standing in my brother's living room, I stared out at the Pacific Ocean. It was so beautiful here and less confining than the east coast. I felt less defined by the specifics of my life. Being here, by myself, was what I needed. I needed time to think, to run, and to sort my thoughts. I saw a new view of my life; the years of validation from a career I appreciated but didn't love. For the past five years, I had been standing neck deep in the world of special needs where I always felt dumb and, more recently, the world of a cancer survivor husband whom I felt isolated from. For the first time in a long time, as I considered these things, I didn't panic. I just felt curious and ready to face it all. I was even oddly calm over the fact that Camp Victory had left me a voicemail. They decided they would not accept Wyatt this summer. Normally I would have invoked Team B, called them up and ripped them a new one, but for some reason I knew it was not a good choice.

My visit with Gabe and Avery, my sister-in-law, had been perfect. They were perfect for each other. I was never happier when he married her. I saw his love for her. I would always see him as the brother who taught me to ride my bike and to read. Gabe was going to be a great dad. My new little nephew Gregory was precious and I silently said a prayer for him to be healthy and neurotypical. My brother is a lot of amazing things, but knowing first-hand the stress of a special needs child, I would never wish that for him.

"Ready to go?" Gabe asked.

Gabe was driving me to the Marriott where the workshop that I had signed up for was being held.

"I am," I said, having no idea what I was ready for.

29| may – june 2018

I was riding down the escalator when my iPhone binged. It was a text from Kelsey. She was a friend of Megan's. Megan had also recruited her to sign up for the workshop. Kelsey and I had exchanged information before I left for California. Kelsey was from Boston, too, and was texting to tell me she was at registration. I smiled, snapped a selfie, and texted it to her as I descended on the escalator, to help us find each other more easily as we had never met.

At the bottom of the escalator ramp, the floor opened up to a large space connecting to a host of conference rooms. There were people everywhere, all ages, ethnicities, and genders. I didn't know what to expect, but I was relieved to see a wide variety of people. On the exterior of one of the conference rooms was a sign, "Basic Registration." *Showtime*, I thought and headed through the open double doors. The registration process was only a sign-in and was not the start of the workshop. We had another thirty minutes before the actual start. I was greeted by bright, shiny people, oozing eagerness to welcome me. I was sure my face was giving one of its not-so- subtle looks, sending out currents like an electric fence, *Stay out of my bubble-space*! I noticed my stomach start to feel a little queasy.

"Melissa!" I heard a female voice call; it was Kelsey. I had just begun to wonder, *What did I sign up for?* Luckily, we found each other almost instantly. A few more minutes and I might have launched the Uber app on my phone, headed back to my brother's home where the comforting views of the Pacific Ocean from the high hills of Palos Verdes would have allowed me to escape my anxiousness. Kelsey and I made our introductions and went about the typical surface talk of strangers; career, where we lived, and how we knew Megan, etc. Kelsey owned her own business in Boston and I could tell she was similar in age to me, another comforting factor. I liked her; she was warm and maybe just as anxious as I was. I looked at my watch--five minutes to start. No leaving now; I was in--at least for day one.

"Ready for this?" I asked.

"Yep!" Kelsey said with a tentative smile. We had determined neither of us knew what we were in for.

Kelsey and I walked into the main conference room where music was blaring and rows of seats were set up lecture style. Once everyone was inside and seated, there were about two hundred people, all of us presumably willing to be transformed. I was skeptical, and I knew one thing for sure . . . this better not be a ton of crying and whining about our parent issues. I was *so* over that bullshit. A memory flashed before my eyes--Tony Robbins' *I Am Not Your Guru*. I had watched it during my "Summer of Netflix and Pringles." I remembered a couple featured on the show, or maybe it was just the husband, howling at the top of his lungs, in front of everyone--I think he was finding his inner animal. I was damn sure *that* was not going to be me.

The double doors to the conference room closed and the music stopped. Seated in the sea of people, I looked straight ahead, and a large sign held a familiar saying: "How you do anything is how you do everything." I knew this saying, I loved it, and more importantly, I wholeheartedly believed it—but I had forgotten it.

***

The verbal agreement all participants give in the workshop is their confidentiality. The workshop is experiential, and it is in the not knowing that creates the most authentic experience for each participant, so for that reason, I will only share what came up for me and how I experienced the workshop.

***

At the close of day one, I glanced at nametags of the new people I had met only hours before as discreetly as possible as I said goodnight using their names. Exiting the conference room I walked with purpose and headed to the elevator. I had one goal in mind: my bed. I was ready for sleep. I had checked into the Marriott where the workshop was being held, knowing that the sessions would be late and quick access to my bed would keep me happy. It was so late. The session had started in the early evening and it was now 11:30 p.m. There were still parts of me feeling like I was on Eastern Time. As I rode the elevator up to my floor I thought a bit about the workshop facilitator, Karen. I wasn't sure I liked her; she was a strange mix of pit bull-aggressive and compassionate like a mother. Ironically, she talked quite a bit about how her passion was rescuing pit bulls. Karen's unexpected quiet tears, showing her compassion and connection when she held space for people's stories was puzzling to me. Or was it impressive?

I got curious--why did I think I didn't like her? Was it really her? Was it the content? Was it possibly the situations being created in the room? So many whys were coming at me. In this one evening, I had heard great stories of inspiration and heartache. Coming to California, I didn't really know what I wanted. I had hoped for space to find myself; I kept saying I was unhappy and lost. But at some point in the evening, a different knowing settled over me. I knew I was more than unhappy. I had lost my joy. I needed to find my joy. I had a feeling my marriage being bumpy was amplified by my joy deficit. I journaled random thoughts for a bit before settling into sleep. I had so many ideas of what might have squashed my joy: work, Jeff's cancer, fear of messing up motherhood, lack of creativity--any and all of it seemed plausible. I turned off my light and went to sleep. I was too tired to think anymore.

The morning brought new clarity on one of my whys as I stood in line at Starbucks waiting to order my latte. I vaguely remembered something Megan had once said to me: *Often what we don't like in others is only a mirror of something we see in ourselves.* I thought about the facilitator again--could this be it? There was no doubt I had a certain aggressive rigidity that could make others uncomfortable. Karen was certainly aggressively rigid. I knew I didn't love this quality about myself. I liked some of the outcomes it had produced in my life, but at what cost? My behavior could leave me feeling like crap. And like a ticker tape crossing the lobes of my brain, a headline appeared: you crave rules, expectations, and control. These rigid ways of living gave me a way to feel good at something, a way to feel good enough, and served as an informal guide to perfection.

My memory of childhood was heavy with rules and expectations--ways to achieve approval and be good enough. My father was impeccable in this way; he followed the rules and was a great provider. He endured long commutes to New York City from Connecticut to support our family. My mother praised my father to us--he was a good man. He sacrificed so much for our family. "Your father never complains. When your father gets home from work, you kids behave," she would say. My father was strong, he did what was expected, he kept his word always, he did what was right, and did it to perfection. As a little girl, I saw my dad as a quiet, stern giant. However, reflecting on my childhood with an adult lens, I saw through the thin disguise. My father carried a lot of pain. Dad grew up in a physically and mentally abusive home raised by his grandparents on their farm in Virginia. He survived an incredibly difficult life. The details which I know of are sparse, but I have always known it has been by the grace of God that my life was more fortunate than his was. I was adopted, *saved*, and raised better. How does one begin to repay such a debt? *Jesus, that's some family baggage*, I thought. So much for *I'm not doing the family and parents* bullshit. I snapped out of my haze and noticed it was my turn to order.

***

During session two with my fellow 200 pre-transformed participants, I sat anxiously in the brightly lit ballroom waiting for the session to begin. I was still mulling over my relationship with rules and what they meant to me and their payoff. What was being created by this very strong preference? I knew the answer right away—inflexibility and a need for perfection. That made me show up as tough to please. I felt my brow furrow. Who would want to be friends with someone like that? Who would want to be married to someone like that? *Oh God, I sucked.*

Our lead trainer appeared at the front of the room. I looked around and spotted various people from my small group. In the previous session, we had been asked to organize ourselves into groups of about eight. The groups were random, with none of us knowing each other. On the surface, we all looked so different from each other, but I had a feeling I was about to know each of them very soon.

***

My small group, as if by divine providence, were meant to be my group. They were my people. We were indeed all very different on the exterior, but the ways in which we connected over the next four days comforted my soul. In the eventual sharing of our stories, some bitter and others beautiful, I experienced boundless compassion and supportive words. These acts of love and generosity became exquisite threads stitching us together, one person to the next. We discovered that we all shared similar stories and or events in our lives. These similarities made me consider new possibilities. Maybe, I was not so different from the rest of the world. Another possibility, the universe had given me what I needed. Or, both could be true.

My stories--my family bullshit and adult shit storm--spilled out in tangled words, far from eloquent, often strangled and almost suffocated by my lack of breath. I was telling secrets. As my words pushed for escape, each word pulled from the pit of my stomach to the top of my throat, disgorged over my lips and out my mouth into the light. There the pain began to lessen, and I began to let it go. I allowed it all to pass through me while holding eye contact without hiding or changing my words to make anyone feel more comfortable. I let my six-year-old self be seen and heard. I let the fearful mother and sad wife be seen and heard.

The voice in my head sneered at me, *Betrayal!* These were our secrets: *If my husband died, who would I be? I would fail at being a mom without him. I couldn't do it on my own. Motherhood had always scared me and it still did. I wasn't good enough. Jeff made me good enough. He made me want to try to be as good and kind as he was; he was so good, so much better than me. I was damaged and less than perfect, and it had been this way forever. Something about me allowed myself to be sexually abused three times by the age of seven. My own mother had said "dirty things" had happened to me. And still I wondered what would she think about the "dirty things" she didn't know that I had to do? Immoral behavior. I remembered hearing these words growing up--this is how sexual behavior was described. I was immoral from the age of five, an unwanted stain. Something about me was damaged and dirty. I would never be as good as everyone else. I could not shake feelings of fear and isolation. I had embarrassed my mom when she asked me to tell one of the boy's mom's what had happened—I couldn't do it, I froze. I failed her.*

These words, my confessions, said out loud, had a duplicitous effect on me. They confused me. I had reasoned a long time ago this line of thinking was not true, but the residue of shame had not been scrubbed away. It was frustrating that I had spent so much time already thinking about my past. When would it be done? At the same time, I couldn't deny my heart had lightened from the relief of letting this out.

In the eyes and faces of my small group seated closely around me in a small circle, I saw and was given compassion, not pity. For years I had mastered talking about what I thought and rarely if ever how I felt. But now my whole truth was out and the fear-hooks were out of me. Fear did not have me anymore. I had it. I began to understand that my relationship with fear could be different. I could decide how to manage it. There were pieces of it I could let go. Finally seeing the source, the place where my destructive beliefs about myself had been built, I could now take care of myself. I saw how I had been wrong. There was nothing wrong with me. Terrible things happened to me, but they were not about me.

I knew that memories could be unreliable, and I had always tried to find comfort in this fact that *maybe* I had gotten some of the memories wrong. But more importantly I believed I was over the physical nature of my abuse. I didn't want anyone to feel sorry for me. I was strong and had moved on, or so I had thought. From within the confines of my small group, it occurred to me that I was still holding in the secret of how the abuse really made me *feel* about myself. This feeling was the source of what I was creating in my life and how I was showing up. In keeping it nameless and denying it light, I gave it power over me. One event or word had the ability to further reinforce its hold and impact, leaving me sad and angry about anything and everything. My secret wasn't that I wanted everything in my life to be perfect, it was that I felt and believed I was imperfect. This heavy feeling had been growing and living in the pit of my stomach for as long as I could remember. This was the nameless battle I was always fighting. But now I knew what *it* was, what I was up against, and this would change everything.

I had gained a small foothold. A place to wrestle back some of my fear and smallness--a way to not let the inner victim win. From this opening, I could be curious. How did I feel about myself when I wasn't blaming or beating myself up? When I chose to be forgiving and loving with myself, what was possible? I had a new lens to see my worthiness. A new lens to see my parents—especially my mother.

The entanglement of being victimized as a child, it's impact, and my relationship with my parents had to be unknotted. They were intertwined and over the years knots of blame, resentment and anger had formed, making a mess.

My new opening was delicate and small, but it was something. I wondered if this opening was like a muscle and over time, it would get bigger and stronger the more I used it. I would *have to* choose this way of thinking. It wouldn't come easy, making the shift from forty plus years of doing and thinking some crazy shit. Everything did not have to be about measuring myself to a level of perfection that I could never realistically achieve, but that always gave me the permission to beat the crap out of myself. Making something my choice gave me a new perspective. Creating my life could be fun, light, and even joyful.

The days in the large conference room rolled from one into the next. As each day passed, the voltage on my electric fence, erected at check-in, lowered until it was turned off. No wall, no barriers, and it occurred to me--I liked myself! I was excited for what was next. For too many years I had handicapped myself and still found a way to accomplish some pretty great things that I was proud of. It could only get better from here.

***

On the last day of the workshop, I stood in my hotel room bathroom and stared into the mirror with lipstick in hand. I looked the same, but I wasn't the same—no, I actually was, I had always been me. It had been as A.J. said it would be; I saw into myself, all of me. And now I got it. I understood how to be the source of my joy. It was always my choice. I only had to choose it and to feel worthy of choosing it.

I looked at my iPhone and selected "Yoga Jan 10," from my music library, one of my old playlists from when I taught yoga. This particular playlist was one of my favorites. It was soulful. "Dust to Dust" by the Civil Wars played in the background. As I continued to get ready for the day, I thought about my life, my story, and the choice to shift. The ways in which I chose to see the machinations of my life could be life-saving. I understood how much power I had over how my story affected me. I could tell the "me-centric" story, the one that focused on shitiness and grand estimations of what the world owed me as I kept a running tab of failed expectations and a laundry list of everyone's imperfections—when in truth I was creating a shield in order to protect myself. Or I could shift my perspective and tell the story of a perfectly imperfect life equipoised with joy and soulful heartache. A life sprinkled with love, challenges, and beautiful friendships found in the most unlikely places. A life that has had the privilege of seeing and being touched by other's vulnerabilities, happiness, and sadness.

It was time to show up like it mattered because it did. The past didn't matter anymore, not in the way it had. My parents had done their best; they had loved me in their best way, but the "family bullshit" was over. Much of it had been out of my control. I could only do my best.

I would probably always feel vulnerable when it came to

parenting my son and that was okay. My love would guide me. I would choose to trust myself day by day. And this was the same with my husband—staying in fear was destructive. Waiting and preparing for another big "gotcha" moment was not living. Looking for ways to control something uncontrollable was distancing me from my joy and a loving marriage. And as much as I loved Jeff and was supported by his love, devotion, and kindheartedness, it dawned on me that I had believed he made me worthy. I had put him on a pedestal of goodness. Jeff was a rule follower not because he feared repercussions but because his moral compass was strong. In contrast to me, Jeff didn't swear, short cuts weren't an option, and he was an engineer on the moral highroad. By association, I felt like I got entrance into the club of the morally-good, which was unfair to both of us. When I faced the possibility of losing him, it was more than losing a life partner—I felt as though I was losing who I was in the world. If Jeff's golden light of goodness didn't shine on me, there would be no light.

The only thing I could do now was live by my values: be vulnerable, passionate, and fearless. I would recognize when the bullshit was taking over and shift out of it by choosing joy instead. It hadn't been lost. I'd work at catching myself building conditions around happiness and instead just allow myself to be happy. The "if then" mentality was really exhausting. Hustling for perfection was another killer of joy.

I was ready for my last day with my 200 now transformed friends. I grabbed my card key, turned off the lights in my hotel room, and headed toward the elevator.

30| june 2018

I arrived home from California jet-lagged, but emotionally energized. I had exhaled fully--body, mind, and heart.

Years ago, Cameron Shayne, the founder of Budokon Yoga, hosted a workshop I attended, and he preached this phrase over and over: "How you do anything is how you do everything." This resonated with me then—the perfectionist in me that is. But during the workshop in California, when this phrase was front and center on the wall it jolted my realization of all the ways I had been showing up like a victim—sad, angry, living in fear. I remembered the Bhakti retreat I had attended a couple of years ago and my first real acknowledgment of how being a victim was showing up in my life. I hadn't stayed in the work; I didn't see how I had been breaking my word to myself. Raghunath had given me a seed to plant within my heart back on that very important morning, but I hadn't realized it was mine to water every day—to tend to its growth. This time would be different. Yes, some hard shit had happened in my life, but that was part of being human and living life, being loved, and loving. Life's bumps would never be my excuse again to be angry and willingly kill my house plant, which when I think about the irony in that, it's equally sad and comical.

At home, I fell back into the folds of my life, picking up Wyatt and arriving at all of our appointments on time. The schedule was the same, but I wasn't the same. As I drove everywhere and tended to the business of our lives, my mind was curious rather than checked-out. I was present. I saw when I chose to act small, be hurt, and let disappointment consume me. That was my old story and I began to *shift*. Life was going to happen as it saw fit and I got to choose how to respond. My job wasn't to come up with an impenetrable plan to control it all. I knew I would never not want to have some kind of plan--I accepted this about myself--but I could now see it had to have more give, leaving room for life's unexpected turns and delights.

***

Slowly, I let go of my finish line mentality toward my marriage. Jeff and I didn't need to reach a milestone of perfection that would signify that we had become awesome or that I was a perfect wife and mother, and my happiness did not depend on this. I had to work on my own joy, mind my own business, and let Jeff care for himself in his own way. He was not mine to control, only to love.

Jeff was still my person. The writing on devotion by Dhanudhara Swami came back to me. I began to realize that so much of what I needed I had all along. I had people in my life advising and supporting me at various times, as far back as college, giving me knowledge and tools on how to get myself out of my deep hole. The California workshop was a bit like a trapper keeper; it organized it all for me in an accessible practical way. I remembered another saying from the workshop that had also been on the wall: "What are you pretending not to know?" I smiled.

It had been summer the day I knew I chose Jeff. I had been so hot, despite wearing a skirt and short-sleeve shirt that day. I met Jeff for lunch at Cosi on Federal Street in Boston. We were dating, on round two actually--we had broken up for three months and recently gotten back together. He had arrived first. Jeff was standing outside Cosi at the top of the steps and as I started to walk up the steps toward him, I saw and felt him see me. Our eyes met and his gaze pulled me in. I was being seen. He didn't look me up and down. When he smiled at me, it grabbed at my heart, and when I smiled in return, I was so filled with happiness I almost laughed out loud. I thought, *He's the one.*

***

I know I'll never completely lose my fear. It compels me to consider perfection as a destination, offering false safety and it's the voice that loves to dress up like anger, sit at my dinner table, and try to run the conversation. Fear talks about not being good enough, it says you'll never belong, and tells me to leave before I'm left, to never be wrong, and that to ask for help is weakness. But the trick I have discovered is that rather than ignore the voice of fear, I give it its say, then move on and choose courage. Courage is one of my best friends; she reminds me I have always belonged and I have been worthy since the day I was born.

I'm ready to move through the hard parts and to experience them without trying to control them. For too long, I have believed that the weight of a single experience would make or break me, but today, I choose a life that plays to my passion rather than ignores it for certainty and this will keep me connected to my joy.

epilogue

I t's been three years since Jeff was diagnosed with colon cancer and we recently marked two years of clean test results. That event changed each of our lives in different ways.

Today I am truly happy and have reconnected to my joy. In the process of coming home back into myself, space has opened up in my heart, leaving room for me to do some much needed work. Jeff and I work at our marriage every day. And in the details of our work I have found my best friend again. Jeff's love still lifts me, but I'm not made important because of it.

These days I compare the beginning of our marriage like driving down a quiet road, where there is no other traffic to watch out for, and the driving is easy. Back then, we were on auto pilot and coasted. But life could not stay static. The road, otherwise known as life, changed, blind spots were added, a few more cars, traffic jams, some pedestrians jay-walking—and if you're driving in India, maybe even an elephant or two. That is our marriage today—full of variety. So we work at staying on the road and not hitting stuff. The drive isn't less wonderful. In fact, it can be amazing, but it's work.

My other work is with my parents, but mostly my mother, whom I love deeply. I am actively working on my relationship with her. Time and mostly my own healing have allowed me to widen my lens and take a new perspective on the possibilities of both my parent's lives. In all of the ups and downs growing up I never felt unloved, just a bit un-liked.

Fair or not, a number of memories are centered around my mom. I think this is because she was at home doing the hard work of raising four children. As a little girl, I had built a story in my head and heart that we were supposed to the Girl Team.

I believe my mother tried the best she could. I see now that for a long time I judged her harshly. And sometimes that judgment came as a consequence of my own harsh self-judgment, but I am done with that. Letting go of the weight and the work of the reinforcing stories, one curated after the next, has allowed me to find happiness in my life. I also believe my mom had her own tribulations to contend with while trying to be the best mom and wife she could. I imagine my mother getting married at nineteen, and I think this would have been hard for so many reasons. But those were different times and not my stories to tell.

This story, these chapters of my life were difficult for me share and feel, but I can finally say I am glad for the lessons; they were a long time coming. Maybe you have found pieces or glimmers of your own story in these pages too. I encourage you, look in the mirror and whisper *into-me-you-will-see* and really look–what do you feel?

###

acknowledgements

I must begin by thanking my husband for being so open, without ego, and supportive of me sharing the details of our life. My story is not mine without him. Jeff always is the first person to believe in me, my dreams, my random ideas, and he often sees my successes before I can.

My parents, I acknowledge and thank them for their bravery, knowing I was writing this story and never once trying to interfere or influence what I might say-- but instead encouraging me.

My mother and father-in-law, there are no words that can ever describe my gratitude. When I thought I might sink, I didn't because you were there, showing me what strength and love looked like in the face of my worst fears.

I owe a special thank you my first read group. Thank you for giving me your precious time. Thank you for supporting me and saying yes, do this! Thank you to my writing partner Neeraj Joshi, your early encouragement gave me the validation I needed to keep going.

A special thank you to Elayne Lieberman, volunteer proofreader. You supported my writing like it was your own.

This story is a snapshot of my life, and there are many people not written about who have supported me, planted seeds, and have helped me to see and become the person I am today. Each of you are my teachers, my family, and dear friends. Thank you for your love, your lessons, your patience; Abe Baron, Chris Barrett, Shiva Bharadwaj, Josh Brown, Dhanurdhara Swami, Chrissy Dhimitri, Kathryn Frias, David Hall, Tam Luc, Deborah Overduput, Puja Puja, Raghunath, Jason Roberts, Nicole Smith, Anthony Tomasi, Anamaria Villamarin, Cleo Villamarin, and Megan Wilson.

Special thank you to my editor Christine Meade, thank you for helping me find more of my story and tidying up my edges.

about the author

Melissa Blaeser is a writer, full-time mom, and retired from Corporate America. For over twenty years, Melissa skillfully performed what felt like a "corporate steeplechase," working in advertising, the dot-coms, and finally software consulting. Life these days consists of the occasional freelance project, a thirteen-year marriage to her husband Jeff, and a full tag-team effort raising their ten-year-old son, who is a Minecraft and Parkour enthusiast. Maintaining balance and space for her personal growth continues to be the underpinning tenant to her happiness. Melissa is currently completing her professional coaching certification. She continues to practice yoga, meditate, and swear like a sailor. Melissa and her family live just north of Boston.

Made in the USA
Middletown, DE
16 July 2020